MALTA

The Triumphant Years
1940–43

MALTA

The Triumphant Years
1940–43

by

GEORGE HOGAN

ROBERT HALE · LONDON

Photoset by Ebenezer Baylis & Son Ltd.,
printed in Great Britain by
Lowe & Brydone Ltd.,
Thetford, Norfolk

DEDICATED

to the Garrison and People of Malta who stood firm, fearless and four-square against a pitiless enemy during the momentous siege years of World War Two. Standing steadfast together in strength of purpose through stress and torment, hunger and peril, linked in humour and friendship, they withstood the terror of continuous bombardment. Their homes fell in ruins and they reeled in the shadow of starvation, yet still their courage grew. From warrior to worker, wife to wee child, each feared the flames yet fought the fire, and as they became bodily weaker through shortage of food, illness and unusual living conditions their will and character expanded through faith. Each one forged a living part of that George Cross which they proudly hold today as a lasting symbol of a mighty task well done.

Contents

Illustrations

10

PICTURE CREDITS

Allied Malta Newspapers Ltd: 1, 2, 6, 7, 26, 27, 28, 29, 30, 32, 33, 34, 35, 36, 38, 40, 41, 42, 46, 51, 53, 54; British Official, Crown Copyright: 3, 5, 8, 9, 10, 11, 12, 13, 14, 15, 16, 17, 18, 19, 20, 21, 22, 23, 24, 25, 31, 37, 39, 43, 44, 45, 47, 48, 49, 50, 52; *Daily Express*: 4; Major George Hogan: 55

Preface

"The use of history is to give value to the present hour and its duty."

EMERSON

The full story of the Great Siege of Malta of 1940–43 can never be written in a popular form. It is too vast. There are many, many stories — dramatic, heroic, mundane, but each an epic in its own right. There are many personal anecdotes, countless relationships and friendships that were surrounded by drama, courage, suffering and pure brotherly love.

There was the strategic angle with Malta a tiny dot in the middle of a vast sea surrounded first by friends and then, at the midnight stroke of a clock in 1940, beset by frenzied, fiendish foes — with no succour for a thousand miles.

There are the stories of the ships: naval cruisers, destroyers, tugboats and the gallant, roving, jolly-roger-flying submarines. Of those merchantmen and tankers who tried and tried again to force their way through blazing, blasted seas against impossible odds to bring aid to a starving people.

Stories, too, of the airmen who started with three obsolescent biplanes for defence and who turned to the offensive as soon as reinforcements arrived. Their lives were forfeit, and they knew it, each time they ventured forth on bombing and torpedo missions. We welcomed the Wellington bombers in and watched in wondering agony as they reduced to six, five, four . . .

And there are stories, too, of the tens of thousands of tons of Axis shipping that the planes and also warships based on Malta did collectively destroy to make an invaluable contribution to the Allied war effort and the destruction of Rommel in Africa.

Stories of the guns and the gunners are still recounted in messes and homes, while the infantry may be remembered as the men in the holes around the airfields and around the coast, firing on low-flying planes, filling in the cratered airfields, rearming and refuelling aircraft for over-stretched, hard-flying fighter pilots, helping the dockies to unload the

ships, setting up smoke screens, building new airstrips and
guarding the old.

Too many stories to contract into one to understand the
true impact. Too many stories to make one cohesive readable
whole. So there will be, and have been, many aspects high-
lighted and some part-truths will be handed down as legends
by word of mouth.

Yet there is one story that does and should supersede
all — the story of the spirit of the people. It shines through the
accounts of ships and planes, of men and guns, of food and
stores. When the normally blue skies were dark with waves of
enemy aircraft and the native honey-coloured rock glowed
faintly through the grey of the bomb-dust and resounded to
the shrill siren, the drone of the Heinkels and the screeching
whistle of the Stukas, the grumbling roar of the Junkers and
pencil-thin Dorniers; then the spirit of the people was as
unflinching as the limestone rock itself and survived an equal
battering.

The crunch and scream of bombs and landmines by day
and night, the blasting of huge buildings and humble dwellings into heaps of rubble, united the population and cemented the desire to defend and retain this loved homeland.

The spirit of the people rose above the paltry facts of life
and there was a four-square approach to living together in
defiance against the adversity created by a ruthless foe. There
was hope and humour, stubbornness and stamina, but above
all there was faith.

The men and women who so rightly and gallantly earned
the George Cross were the parents of children who knew
nothing but siege conditions. Those youngsters now have children of their own. It is partly for them and their children's
children that I have recalled these episodes which, I hope,
make a balanced account of those fateful years and have
included some of the verses I wrote then anonymously as
'The Captain'. Together I believe they express the atmosphere of those days of peril, courage and perseverance.

Those were heart-aching days when deliverance seemed
far, far off, but when life was the more sweet because living
was so dangerous, when pettiness was forgotten as disaster
struck all round and when each man's task was seen to be an
essential part of the whole nation's ability and will to survive.

Never before in history had a garrison the responsibility for such a large number of civilians within a besieged fortress. The few thousand British servicemen and women who, with the Maltese soldiers, made up that garrison, and the merchant seamen who so heroically brought in the needed supplies, will long remember Mother Malta. I hope this record, with the verses we knew then, will help their children, too, to understand.

Only the spirit of the people enabled the garrison to tackle, to continue and to complete its task unhampered and with unqualified success. Had the faith behind the spirit faltered, the people themselves would have died. Had Malta fallen, the North African campaign might never have ended in victory for the Allies. Certainly the war would have lasted years longer and, many believe, could well have been lost.

The story also shows that the thoughts of besieged Malta were by no means all inward, there was no self-pity. The 8th Army in North Africa, the invasions of Sicily and Normandy, the heroic merchant seamen and European refugees were all in the thoughts of Malta. For as Malta endured, Malta could understand. There was true realization of the struggles and sufferings of others and that the island's role was part of a world-wide strategy.

I hope this account will bring to life for those who were there and for many others the colourful, dramatic but intensely human story that was Malta's glory.

This book is the result of personal observations and recollections, but to refresh my memory in order to fill out the background I have looked again at accounts of the siege in contemporary records such as Leslie Oliver's *Malta Besieged* (Hutchinson), Francis Gerard's *Malta Magnificent* (Cassell), Sybil Dobbie's *Grace Under Malta* (Lindsay Drummond), Flying Officer George F. Beurling and Leslie Robert's *Malta Spitfire* (Hutchinson) and many cuttings from the *Times of Malta* and *The Sunday Times of Malta* which I collected at the time and have cherished over the years. I have also studied the official accounts produced as the conflict was ending and immediately afterwards, such as *The Air Battle of Malta*, *The Mediterranean Fleet*, *East of Malta, West of Suez*, *Fleet Air Arm* and *Merchantmen at War* (all

H.M.S.O.). Where I have found 'facts' at variance (censorship was very strict at the time and some 'cover' may have been necessary when war still raged), I have sought for the truth, knowing that myth and legend can derive from any statement often enough repeated. I have also looked again at T. Zammit's *Malta—The Islands and Their History* published in 1929, and am grateful for remembrances recovered when looking through Charles J. Boffa's *The Second Great Siege*. The more recently published *Panzer Army Africa* by James Lucas (Macdonald and Jane's and *The Trail of the Fox* by David Irving (Weidenfeld and Nicolson), confirmed for me the German viewpoint that we appreciated at the time—their determination to 'take out' Malta and, what is not always credited, the island's most effective part in the restriction of Rommel's campaign.

Also I am indebted to the Burke Publishing Company for permission to use extracts from General Dobbie's introduction to *Britain's Conquest of the Mediterranean* published in 1944; to the *Sunday Express* for permission to use extracts from an article mentioning Lord Gort by the late John Gordon, then editor, and published in that newspaper in 1944 and for permission to reproduce a cartoon by Strube published in the *Daily Express* in 1942. Also to the Air Historical Branch of the Royal Air Force for aid in listing the air squadrons in Malta during the siege and to other friends and helpers for their assistance. Many of the photographs come from the war album of Allied Malta Newspapers, others are Crown Copyright and were either passed to me during the war years or are loaned from the photographic library of *Soldier* Magazine.

To all: many thanks, not only for bringing the past to light but for stirring that computer we call memory to recreate many experiences and stories we once knew so well but which had receded almost into oblivion.

G.R.H.

ONE

Bomb-Drop

The Italian heavy bomber planes flew high overhead in exact formation. In the bright morning sunlight they looked like shining silver specks as they progressed slowly, steadily and deadly straight on their bombing run southward towards Luqa airfield. The anti-aircraft shells were bursting in all too few patterns below and behind them. A hundred or so shirt-sleeved Maltese stood watching in a massed group outside a deep rock shelter on the high ground at St James's Cavalier in Valletta just fifty yards from the Auberge Castile, then the headquarters of the British troops in Malta.

The Castile Square was empty except for a lone figure by the Garrison Church, hard by the Upper Barrakka. He was quite unconcerned, just leaning over the stone parapet looking into the Grand Harbour. A naval officer was moving smartly but unhurriedly down the steps that led to the Royal Navy's underground operations room at Lascaris.

From the gardens of the Barrakka there was a fine view over the best harbour in Europe, the shipping in the creeks to the east and south and the historic Three Cities that flanked them. Vittoriosa, Cospicua and Senglea had already taken a heavy battering from the Luftwaffe when the badly crippled aircraft carrier H.M.S. *Illustrious* had sought refuge and repairs a few weeks earlier in January 1941.

The German aircraft had come to avenge the victory at Taranto—the destruction of Italy's capital ships by the Swordfish planes of *Illustrious*. The Junkers and Stukas had caught her at sea, singled her out and had tried so hard to sink her and had failed. Now they failed again when she was stationary in harbour but their bombs had created havoc in the Three Cities. *Illustrious* had slipped away to Alexandria and would refit in America, she was so badly damaged, but her survival was a sign to the Maltese, in spite of their own deep wounds and the mass evacuations that the week-long blitz had caused.

A sign that tenacity, perseverance, courage, doggedness

would succeed. The success of *Illustrious* at Taranto had also been a sign. Mussolini, who had declared that Italy would be non-belligerent, had cringed to the Führer when German troops were all-conquering and France was about to fall. Not only that, his first warlike act was to strike at tiny Malta with eight frightening raids on the first day. The success of *Illustrious* at Taranto had been a sign that we could strike back.

But to return to the watchers by St James's Cavalier. The Hampshire Regiment had reached Malta some twenty-four hours earlier and this was our first sight of the slow-moving, high-flying Italian bombers—too high to be accurate, some said. The shells burst spectacularly but harmlessly and, to us on the Castile Square, it all seemed somewhat remote. I had charge of an Army pick-up, had drawn stores from the NAAFI at St James's and should now make my way back some four miles south to my company by the little San Loretto Chapel at Gudja, near Luqa airfield—the apparent destination of the bombers.

The Maltese, hesitant about going into the shelter, waited patiently, looking at the planes and wondering when the all-clear would sound. There appeared to be little local danger. "Load up!" I told the quartermaster, and away we went. We had driven less than a mile and had just passed the outer city gates, the Portes Des Bombes, when I spotted another wave of aircraft on the bombing run, slowly but unerringly coming up behind us—and we, invitingly, were the only thing moving on that long, open road.

Even as I spotted them there came the whistle and scream of a heavy missile rushing through unresisting air and a shattering explosion disintegrated the ground just ten yards to the right of the truck. "Keep going!" I yelled, quite unnecessarily, and as the truck leapt forward with full acceleration fragments of the bomb hopped, slithered and ricocheted for some 200 yards along the downhill road behind us. Fortunately it had fallen on sloping ground beyond the verge and we had not received the direct blast. Our speed, too, saved us from the splinters, but only just. We stopped and I picked up a piece of the iron casing that had danced along beside us. It was still hot, too hot to hold, and I felt some respect for the bomber who had obviously let one go early—about three miles early. Just for laughs? Bombing is usually a communal experience but this was personal.

This was our introduction, as infantrymen from the North African desert, to Italian high-level bombing—the planes slow, in exact drill formation, but oh, so accurate. What would it be like just sitting in slit trenches around an aerodrome with no chance individually of hitting back? The ack-ack seemed ineffective at that height and there were so few fighter planes on the island. What was it like for the Maltese countryfolk just sitting in their houses and their shelters in the village right by the side of the Luqa airfield?

Later we would know Kesselring's Junkers that would keep us occupied by day and by night, the screaming Stuka dive-bombers that were aimed directly at the target and pulled up only at the last moment to let the bombs away—unless they were hit, when they, too, came on down to crash on to the target. Even the Messerschmitts with cannons and machine-guns spattering at military targets and anything else that moved or displeased them. They were especially nauseous when our gunners had nothing or next to nothing left to fire back at them. We would learn to treat with respect, too, the guns of our own Spitfires lest they be chasing at house-top height some enemy plane that had sneaked in under the radar screen.

But this was early in 1941 when the great blitz was yet to come, when the enormous destruction of houses and palaces, farmsteads and churches, could not be envisaged; the time before the effects of continuous hunger had yet to undermine the physique, before malnutrition and unusual living conditions had brought disease and, almost but not quite, despondency.

This, too, was before anger, determination, courage and pure faith had built up the spirit of the people into the glory of the story behind Malta's George Cross. For there was something about the Maltese that nurtured a reserve of stamina and doggedness and produced an inherent dry wit that bolstered their resistance and enabled them to withstand adversity even as it gradually became more restrictive and enervating. A humour so well expressed in the vernacular but hard to interpret.

Here was a spirit that said in effect: "This is my homeland, do what you dare but here I stay. Pound, slay, destroy; when you have vented your anger you will go. Surely there will be retribution much harder for you to endure. Here I remain." And they had remained on this tiny island in the midst of a vast sea surrounded by many nations; outliving predators and overlords, even the bold Phoenicians, the warlike Romans, the long-staying Arabs, the Normans, the Aragonese, the noble Knights, the French, and defying and beating off the ambitious and far-conquering Turks.

FAITH AND ENDURANCE

In the far-off days of the great forays
When the bold Phoenician roamed,
When the Greek ran wild and the Roman smiled
And the sea by Carthage foamed,
We prayed a prayer in our direst need
To the God we had come to know:
"Our trust in Thee for us and our seed,"
While our warriors fought each foe.

The centuries have drifted by
And Carthage fell in flame;
But still are we in the Middle Sea,
And our Island rock the same,
And our Island men of the same old breed
With the same old family tie
And *"Our trust in Thee for us and our seed"*
The same familiar cry.

In the days of the Great Siege of World War II the 30,000 British and Maltese garrison and 255,000 Maltese civilians stood four-square to meet the onslaught of the Axis forces. The island, strategically well placed on the direct route from Italy to Libya, could, if well supplied and garrisoned, prevent Axis reinforcements reaching North Africa. Malta's position midway between Gibraltar and Port Said enabled the British Mediterranean Fleet, whose peacetime headquarters it was, to keep open the route to the east through the Suez Canal.

The strategy was simple in 1939 with Malta safe and far from any likely trouble. France was friendly, Italy neutral and, said Il Duce, intending to remain so. The Mediterranean was still blue and free with a golden sun unshadowed by black bombers and grey bomb-dust. But there were dark clouds gathering beyond the horizon and, unexpectedly, Malta's days of destiny were soon to dawn. A new testing time would open, a formidable challenge was building up and a daunting task would have to be tackled. But first let me tell you a little about this fascinating and historic isle and the early growth of the people.

TWO

In the Beginning

In the beginning was the island and the island was of lime-stone. But before the beginning, in a time that cannot be remembered, the sabre-toothed tiger, the hippopotamus and the dwarf elephant roamed a vast land that stretched far north into Italy and south into Africa. Before the centuries could be counted the earth became covered with ice and when the ice melted the vast Middle Sea was formed and there was the island. And the men who walked on the island were the first of the Maltese race.

Knowledge of those first fathers is forgotten, too. The memory cannot cast back 6,000 years or 40,000 years, but some time in this period the first Maltese men appeared and they spoke with a Semitic tongue, to which all future callers made contribution but did not mongrolize. There was a time when they stood together at their temples at Hagar Qim, as their cousins did at England's Stonehenge, and they stood together, too, at Mnaidra and at Ggantija in Calypso's isle of Gozo. Also there was a time when they knew the mysteries of the Hypogeum at Paola. But those days are long, long gone.

What is remembered is the warm, rich sun shining from a blue sky on to the deep blue waters where the fish were easy prey and bountiful—the clear, inviting waters round the island of rocky limestone. There were few trees and little earth but in due season the verdant areas brought forth cactus and fruit and roots for sustenance. The people, who were few, lived in peace, content with their prickly pears, olives, citrus, grapes and pumpkins, goats and fish.

The limestone, soft and white in the earth, was as beautiful as the maidens and the men fashioned it easily and built their homes. In the sun-drenched air it hardened and mellowed to the colour of the island honey, and the dust and the chippings of the building were trodden back into the earth to become the goodly surface of the country roads.

As man returns to dust and new birth perpetuates the race, so the dust of the limestone remoulds and never dies. And as

man is dust, so in Malta man and limestone are one. Hard
when weathered, tough and unbreakable. When beaten
down will never die but remoulds to rebuild and rise again.

A BIRTHRIGHT

If you take a bit of limestone and you pound it with a rod
It takes a lot of beating ere you break it,
And if you take the dust of it and press and pound and prod
You'll find you'll not destroy it, but remake it.

If you look into the sunflower you will see the eyes of man,
In the open rolling country find the breast of him,
And dancing through the daisies with the same swift feet as
Pan
Come the little bits and pieces for the rest of him.

The roistering winds of springtime imbue him with their
breath,
The age-old stones their wisdom freely scatter,
But the will that takes him onward through all fevers to his
death
That is fashioned from the rocky limestone matter.

You may take that living limestone and may pound it with
a rod,
It takes a lot of beating ere it's crumbled;
And after death the dust of it is pounded, pressed and trod
To remake it, for it's never, never humbled.

So Mother Malta lived in freedom in the middle of the
Middle Sea while other nations rowed their galleys around
the long Mediterranean coasts, trading and fighting,
conquering and plundering. Soon they visited and coveted
Malta. The Phoenicians came about 1,000 years before
Christ was born and they liked what they saw and stayed. The
Romans came in 218 B.C., but a miracle that lives in the
island's memory was the night of the great storm when Paul
of Tarsus and Luke, prisoners under Roman guard among a
ship's company of 276, were shipwrecked on the way to
Rome.

During his enforced three months' stay on the island Paul persuaded the people to Christianity and baptized the island's chief citizen, the Roman Governor Publius of Floriana, to become Malta's first high priest in the Lord. Another eleven centuries passed and the Arabs took over and stayed for 200 years. Then came the Normans and the Aragonese, but patiently through it all the Maltese race survived.

Came the time of the Crusades when Europe was concerned for its own safety and the survival of Christendom. Then the withdrawal of the Knights of Jerusalem from the Holy Land to Cyprus, Rhodes and Viterbo in Rome province, until in 1530 they were to take up residence in Malta, to build their *auberges* for the different nationalities in the Order and to stand guard at this strategic point covering southern Europe.

In 1565 the Turks attacked and the first Great Siege of Malta began. The Knights and Maltese stubbornly demonstrated their powers of endurance, stamina and ferocity and set standards of courage and tenacity that the present-day islanders still applaud and commemorate annually. The Turks were thoroughly defeated after a most bloodthirsty encounter, losing 20,000 of the 30,000 who had landed. This was more than a repulse, more than a great victory for a tiny island. Malta had saved Europe by her determination and bravery—even as she was to do again nearly four centuries later. By accident or Almighty design the central position has ensured Malta strategic importance throughout the ages.

Two more centuries passed and the French were the new masters. Napoleon visited the island and took surrender from the Knights, but the French were arrogant and grasping and the Maltese were soon in revolt and urgently imploring Nelson to assume control. The French were besieged in Valletta by the Maltese on land and the British fleet at sea and the patriot Vincent Borg, popularly called Braret and later knighted, ran up the British flag at Birkirkara on 9 February 1799, anticipating the close bond that was to last more than a century and a half. He did not wait for Nelson's authority but the Admiral acceded to his letters of entreaty by sending one of his captains, Alexander Ball, who was appointed President of the Provisional Government later that year.

Among the many incidents of those days was one that echoed a name 141 years later almost to the hour. During the night of 25 July 1800 the French frigate *Diana* slipped out of Grand Harbour to seek help from France and was captured by Nelson's blockading force. Oddly the name *Diana* dramatically reappears in Malta's story in 1941 when on the night of 25–26 July an Italian warship of that name lay-to nine miles off the coast to instigate a daring raid on Grand Harbour. We shall hear more of this in a later chapter. Neither of these vessels, named after the goddess of the chase who was associated so appropriately with the moon and the power to send sudden death, was fleet enough to outwit the Maltese and British in close unity. Another striking historical duplication also had birth during that night of 1800, for it was the British fast frigate *Penelope* that played a dramatic part in chasing and holding *Diana* and three other French vessels that accompanied her, including two battleships. In 1942 another *Penelope* endowed with equal dash, determination and courage would also achieve great renown at Malta.

After the defeat of the French the Maltese cemented their friendship with Britain and during the next 140 years the ties between the two nations grew strong. Malta became the headquarters of the British Mediterranean Fleet. In the nineteenth and twentieth centuries the Grand Harbour, Marsamxett with its submarine base, and Sliema Creek were impressive and satisfying sights with the long lines of light grey battleships, cruisers and destroyers that watched over the trade routes to the East and helped to keep the *Pax Britannica* on the seven seas.

The economy of the island prospered, benefiting from the large number of servicemen—an Army garrison as well as the Naval force—and the dockyard and coaling facilities. Along the Gzira waterfront the sailors' rendezvous even served English fish and chips.

The people lived happily and multiplied more quickly than in earlier centuries and they visited daily their splendid parish churches, the focal point of their existence and their intense pride—the parish priest being their mentor and friend. They assimilated British ideas but strongly retained their own nationality, jealously guarding their rights and beliefs and nurturing their aristocracy whose families are among the oldest in Europe. They held feast days throughout the year so that at almost every weekend one village or another was parading the huge statue of its patron saint and celebrating with much jollity and brilliant firework displays.

English became the language of law and commerce and there was much inter-marriage. The regular gunner regiment found a place in the British Army List and both this unit and the part-time infantry battalion were proud to receive the Sovereign's approval when designated the Royal Malta Artillery and the King's Own Malta Regiment. Malta was gaining in prosperity and growing apace when World War Two opened.

THE SENTINELS: 1941

We stand where our fathers stood,
We stand and we shall not fail,
While the light rays search and the buildings lurch,
We stand through the shrapnel hail.

We watch while our comrades sleep,
We scan both the sea and the skies,
We watch in the dark, in the dusk, at the dawn,
And never sleep wearies our eyes.

We are brothers in arms are we:
My brother he lends me his ear,
I lend him my eyes and together we see;
United we stand without fear.

We stand where our fathers stood,
We stand and await the gale,
Though the night be still and the prospect good.
If we sleep—then Freedom fail.

THREE

Position Central

When war between Britain and Germany was declared on 3 September 1939 Malta was happily positioned far from the area of likely intense hostilities and almost dead centre in the friendly Mediterranean Sea. The entire coastline was either neutral or under Allied influence. How much safer could any island feel, noting the non-aggressive nations around her? From Gibraltar round Spain, France, Italy, Yugoslavia, Albania, Greece, Turkey, Syria, Palestine, Egypt, Libya, Tunisia and the whole of the North African seaboard round again to Gibraltar.

The British and French navies shared the guardianship of this huge sea. So when much of the Royal Navy was necessarily called home for service around Britain's coasts, in the North Sea, the Channel and the Atlantic, it was strategically correct for Admiral Sir Andrew Cunningham to move the remainder of his Mediterranean command to Alexandria. He left Force K, consisting of two cruisers and two destroyers, and the Nth Submarine Flotilla at Malta. The island was in no danger, especially as Mussolini had declared that the Italians would remain neutral.

The entry into the war on 10 June 1940 of Italy and the totally unforeseen capitulation of France fifteen days later entirely changed the situation. The whole Mediterranean strategy collapsed and Malta was immediately placed in a precarious position. The vast Mediterranean, over 2,000 miles from west to east with Malta midway, now became the responsibility of those reduced naval forces remaining under Admiral Cunningham. Moreover, the French fleet, which had shared the guardianship, was now a potential and strong adversary.

The friendly coasts around the Mediterranean at once bristled with hostility and Malta was open to attack and siege, with ambitious Mussolini's Regia Aeronautica free to bomb from bases barely sixty miles to the north in Sicily and his swaggering navy ready to assume control of what the

Italians called *Mare Nostrum*, Our Sea. While Malta's land garrison could be expected to hold out for some time, the small naval force required supplies, especially masses of fuel, to remain offensive. There would be some difficulty in getting supplies 1,000 miles through a hostile sea, either from Gibraltar in the west or Port Said in the east. Whichever way the Maltese looked it was a long, long way to a friendly shore and there was never any hope of quick help. Here on the island it was necessary to sustain nearly 300,000 people whose farmers grew less than one-third of the food the island needed, who kept no cattle for meat or milk, relying on the goat for milk and cheese, and who were even short of water except in very rainy winters.

As well as the need for a continuing supply of food and materials for the populace there was also the vital necessity to bring in fuel, ammunition and armaments for the defending garrison — a defence that would need to be well bolstered if the island was to remain effective.

There was one other vital deficiency in this island standing alone — if it was to stand and survive — there were no aerial defenders. None, that is, except 'Faith', 'Hope' and 'Charity', three obsolescent Gloucester Gladiator biplanes found in packing cases at the Fleet Air Arm base at Kalafrana after the departure of the aircraft carrier H.M.S. *Glorious*.

From the remoteness of today and, more especially at that vital moment in history, there is and was a glaring and angry question-mark. As the Maltese were looking anxiously skywards they were asking: "Why was Malta left so pitifully unprotected?"

But more. Before the cases could be unpacked and the machines assembled, signals had to be passed to higher authority for permission. Then the planes were made ready, but even as they were being inspected another order came to countermand the first and they were repacked. It was some time before more red tape was eventually cut and the craft finally assembled. Then there were no crews, so six volunteer pilots of the Royal Air Force were hurriedly trained and Malta's 'first of the few' were ready like ancient charioteers to battle with and beat off the whole might of Il Duce's sophisticated Regia Aeronautica. Originally there were four Gladiators but only three were ever seen in the air together. They were known for a time as 'Pip', 'Squeak' and 'Wilfred', and as 'Freeman', 'Hardy' and 'Willis', like the cartoon characters or the 'shoebox' assemblies they at first might have seemed to be. But as they survived and prospered against odds, the Maltese called them almost naturally 'Faith', 'Hope' and 'Charity', which fitted them so well and signified the feelings of those who watched their tremendous efforts and hair-raising exploits.

As for the British Mediterranean Fleet, the world now knows how Admiral Cunningham's immediate decisive actions and aggressive spirit, combined with the courage, stubbornness and stamina of his captains and men, kept the Italians at bay and coped brilliantly with a complex situation.

After the crippling raid by Swordfish aircraft from the carrier *Illustrious* on the Italian capital ships at Taranto on 11 November 1940 and the great sea victory of Matapan, 27–30 March 1941, Mussolini's fleet never challenged again; but with fast warships and hordes of aircraft they were still a dire menace to slow-moving convoys and it was a long, hard struggle to keep Malta supplied and defended.

Malta, nearly a thousand miles from the main Mediterranean Fleet, was also on the direct route to Italy's North African colonies but, thought Il Duce, and Hitler too, this speck could easily be reduced, devastated or even captured. A softening-up process had been begun before the war through a friendly 'seduction' method of free youth trips and other excursions, aimed, many believed, at bringing Malta within the Italian fold. There are many Maltese of Italian descent on the island, but, indeed, there are also many descended from noble families from other old kingdoms of Europe. There was some sympathetic leaning towards Italy but, in the event, Mussolini's contemptuous betrayal and the immediate appearance of his bombers with eight horrific raids on the first day at once turned any tolerance into disgust and loathing.

From Alexandria Cunningham wasted no time and after 'trailing his coat' and enticing the Italians to defeat at Matapan set about to effectively control the Mediterranean. With the relatively small force under his command this was no longer fully possible, but with ships, troops and planes of the three services co-ordinating magnificently the enemy was harassed and the Germans were forced to withdraw troops from other fronts to support Mussolini in Greece and North Africa. Also they based a large portion of the Luftwaffe in Sicily to support Rommel and his supply routes and to endeavour to subdue and then to attempt to annihilate Malta.

From the island itself cruiser Force K and the Nth Submarine Flotilla struck swiftly and surely, repeatedly and continuously harassing the enemy's line of communication between Italy and North Africa. Royal Marines were posted ashore to man guns at Kordin and on the headquarters 'stone frigate' H.M.S. *St Angelo.* The Force K cruisers *Aurora* and *Penelope* with destroyers *Lively* and *Lance* came and went, and the highly successful submarines were absent from the island for weeks on patrol, raiding and sinking, observing and bringing in supplies and mail. Every Maltese knew when they were in and what they had accomplished and it was a sad day when they eventually withdrew to operate from a better supply base in Egypt.

The Maltese knew then that their backs were really hard set against the wall of rock that their ancestors, too, 375 years earlier, had defended so stubbornly.

Over 2,250,000 tons of enemy shipping were sunk in the Mediterranean in the three years to the beginning of 1943, much of it by the centrally positioned, Malta-based air and sea forces. To put Malta's strategic importance in some perspective, may it be recorded that the enemy shipping sunk in the same period in the North Sea, along the coasts of Norway, east and west of Denmark and in the English Channel, totalled 1,100,000 tons.

Also to show in true light the intensity of bombardment and the defensive necessity and ability of the island, the following figures of aerial results are enlightening:

Over Britain in 1942 there were 738 enemy aircraft destroyed for the loss of 544 Allied pilots and 593 planes. Over tiny Malta during the same period 915 enemy planes were destroyed against the loss of 106 pilots and 195 planes. Of these the Royal Air Force destroyed 733 enemy aircraft and also probably destroyed another 216. The guns alone brought down 182.

These figures are quoted merely to illustrate the intensity of the bombardment and the continued harassment of a people on a tiny, densely populated, leaf-shaped island seventeen miles by eight — smaller than the Isle of Wight. An island of rock where the reverberations of every one of those thousands of tons of bombs could be felt by all.

The bombing of Malta was more intense than the bombing of London and there were longer periods of intensity. In the first 205 days of 1942 London had 57 consecutive days of air attacks; in that same period Malta's bombardment went on for 154 consecutive days without let-up. In the first 180 days of 1942 there was only one raid-free day — it was too stormy. We are not looking for records but noting agony, and it is fair to point out that incendiaries caused immense fires that gutted London but had little effect on Malta. There are few trees on Malta and the houses are stone built without wooden structures. Therefore, more high explosives were dropped on Malta and the big stone blocks from the thick walls and roofs blocked roads to produce huge mountains of rubble. One important visitor said the enormous destruction reminded him of the devastation he had seen at Arras and Ypres in the First World War.

But the people did not cower under the bombardment. They were amazed and fearful, but they were angry with the duplicity of the Italians and they found determination and the will to resist and exist through stubbornness and faith. More and more through faith.

STEADFAST SENTINEL

Weep not a tear for that fair Isle,
Breathe not a sigh, turn not a hair.
Let the mad Boche despise, revile;
Malta is standing sentinel there.

Look at the shoals around the coast!
Look at the cliffs! Look at the rock!
Heard you the Hun, his early boast?
Malta can still withstand his shock.

What is that silvery flashing dart
Under the water? Out to the deep
Moving and searching, playing a part,
Turning and coming back home to sleep.

While out in the dark, deserted, red,
Blazing and burning, bursting and done,
Its foolish escort maimed and bled,
Just one more ship of the war-mad Hun.

What are those wild birds flashing by?
Score upon score, sombrely dressed.
Heavy their load when away they fly;
Gaily and lightly back to their nest.

While away to the north a flaming roar
With blood red tears fills Italy's cup;
And away to the south a battered Korps
Thankfully watches the sun come up.

What do you see when you reach the coast? —
Only a friend can approach with ease —
Eyes upon eyes, a sleepless host,
Rank upon rank and a flag in the breeze.

What is it makes this gem so pure?
Not the wild birds, not the bright dart,
Not the clear eyes — they too endure —
But each man playing his own small part.

Cast not a tear for that fair Isle,
Breathe not a sigh, turn not a hair.
Let the mad Boche despise, revile;
Malta is standing sentinel there.

FOUR

First Sight

The 1st Battalion Hampshire Regiment which had been in the desert at Mersa Matruh and other points along the North African coast left Alexandria for Malta on 21 February 1941 in His Majesty's cruisers *Orion* and *Ajax*, escorted by destroyers *Jaguar* and *Wolf*. Also aboard was the 2nd Battalion Cheshire Regiment — a unit of machine gunners. In Alexandria harbour we saw the badly battered aircraft carrier *Illustrious* of Taranto fame.

We expected to have to run the gauntlet to the island and wondered how the unloading would go. After all, a whole battalion concentrated with all its armament, equipment and stores on board ship is a much easier target than the same unit dispersed on land. We mounted our own machine-guns as extra anti-aircraft protection — just in case.

With speed as one of the essentials for surprising and eluding the enemy, the warships made a rapid passage of thirty-six hours for the 820 miles, arriving in Grand Harbour on the morning of 23 February without spotting one enemy plane. From seaward in the early morning sunlight the huge, high, dominating bulk of Valletta, the city fortress built by Grand Master La Vallette after the 1565 siege, shone golden and looked impregnable. So it had done to Napoleon and to Nelson in their turn. The watch-towers at St Elmo Point and further in at Senglea, with their distinctive eye and ear adornments, stood out like alert sentinels — which, indeed, they were and had been for nearly four centuries. Salutes were exchanged with the 'stone frigate' H.M.S. *St Angelo*, the Naval headquarters, and I stood down the gun that my company had mounted on *Ajax*.

We made our way ashore across a huddle of lighters supporting an undulating timber road without the inconvenience of an air raid. Few ships, then or later, achieved this freedom and we wondered if our luck would hold. Quickly we loaded our transport and were on our way to the village of Gudja some four miles southward and hard by the extended airfield of Luqa. What little we saw of the inhabitants that day showed them to be friendly and extremely helpful.

The women were mostly dressed in black and the faldetta headdress was much in evidence in the country areas. The girls and children were wide-eyed and beautiful. The men were all in shirtsleeves, they never wore coats, only waistcoats, but these were country folk. Our rather rough quarters included many small outbuildings previously occupied by goats and hens. The Army never ousted tenants from their houses but accepted what was vacant and paid for the privilege. The Air Force always had better quarters than the Poor Bloody Infantry, while the Americans when they eventually came to Gozo just took what they wanted and flattened everything else that was in the way.

Battalion headquarters was in Ix-Xlejli Tower with its beautiful walled garden—the colonel and his staff being privileged to enjoy the same views that Napoleon is reputed to have seen during his week's stay in 1798. They may not have had as many lice and fleas as we found in our humble stone shacks but they possibly attracted more bombing. Nevertheless, Ix-Xlejli Tower was never destroyed and still stands today. No doubt it was an excellent landmark for attacking planes and better intact than demolished.

The 2nd Devonshires and 1st Dorsets shared our Southern Infantry Brigade, later to become Montgomery's famous 231 (Malta) Brigade and selected for particular independent tasks. The Northern Infantry Brigade held the other half of the island.

The overall and immediate task of the Hampshires was the defence of the southern dispersal areas of Luqa airfield, while the Queen's Own Royal West Kents watched the main runways. But the Hampshires were also available and prepared for many roles including mobile reserve and coast defence, and undertook bicycle patrols and intensive training. Our company areas also included Zurrieq, Mqabba and the Safi air strip, which the battalion, and C Company in particular, took a great part in clearing, building and defending. One road junction here was named quite naturally King's Cross after the company commander, Reg King, who later was awarded the Military Cross and joined the New Zealand forces after the War.

The George Cross, and
King George's citation

"This scorpion, this Malta . . ." Like a silver leaf on an azure sea

INDELIBLE

Hitler, Goering and Mussolini. A Strube cartoon in the *Daily Express*, 14 May 1942

Lone raider by moonlight

Part of the Grand Harbour barrage with tracer intermingled and emphasized in a time-exposed photograph. Something, probably a ship, is well alight beyond the building

Looking south-west from Valletta, with the ramparts in the foreground. The searchlights are focusing in one area. A crashed plane burns fiercely on the left and another in the distance beyond the damaged St Publius Church, Floriana

An aerodrome in Malta, with Spitfires on the ground and a Beaufighter coming in to land

Soldiers fitting fuses and tail fins to bombs

A Bren gun carrier being used for towing trolley loads of bombs to the dispersal points

Soldiers and airmen worked together to refuel and reload planes, getting them into the air in record time

Their day starts at first light with a stand-to

Ack-ack crew at gun-stations

A troop commander supervises gun drill

Heavy 'AA' guns in action during a raid

The Combined Operations room where Army, Navy and R.A.F. worked together

Air Vice Marshal Sir Keith Park, A.O.C. Mediterranean, talking with men of a Malta bomber crew who had distinguished themselves in operations, 18 January 1943

To visitors from Britain today, who usually arrive in the heat of high summer, Malta looks barren, sun-scorched and even unkempt with its uneven dry-stone walls, straggling cactus, lack of grass and dearth of trees. That is, to visitors from the luscious green of Britain with its luxuriant grass, tall pines, oaks and birches, and its field-enclosing hedges. To us Poor Bloody Infantry from the desert, with its undulating expanses of sand from horizon to horizon, Malta appeared as it must have looked to those early Arabs and Moors, a haven of comparative grandeur, especially in the spring of the year with grass in the low-lying Marsa area and bright yellow chrysanthemums in a profuse mass of full bloom all the way from Portes des Bombes to Pieta Creek.

The solid limestone houses of the villagers with pumpkins ripening in the sun on the flat roofs, colourful washing there, too, gave promise of companionship after the bleak months in North Africa where even the nomads ceased to roam. There were crops in the tiny fields surrounded by the never-ending lines of stone walls, and fig trees and olives as well as orange and lemon orchards.

We had to get used to this new terrain — and quickly, in case of invasion — and when we were not mounting Bren guns from slit trenches around the airfields and our own particular villages, we were leaping the walls and seeking out alternative routes in readiness.

The houses of the islanders are all built of the native limestone and our area included many of the quarries from which the two-cubic-foot blocks were excavated. Some of these quarries were huge and some were not easily discernible, especially in half light. Many a man was saved only in the nick of time from jumping a low stone wall in the exuberance of a mock charge to fall twenty feet, even forty feet, into oblivion. One or two actually disappeared temporarily, but survived.

Water was brought to us daily in huge casks on donkey carts, for there was little tap supply and most houses had a surface-draining well. These, too, were distinctive in the fields, each with a stone arch extending six feet above ground level to support the bucket rope. Another outstanding feature was the wayside shrine, each with a small statue of a patron saint. These can be seen on country roads, especially at junctions, and on walls of houses in villages and towns.

At the crossroads between Mqabba and Luqa were the twin statues of St Peter and St Paul with vases of flowers that were often renewed. The dispersal area for Luqa airfield was adjacent and the Junkers roared in over the crossing to bomb the airfield. Inevitably some bombs fell short and this was not a place to be caught in when the alert sounded, but St Peter and St Paul survived for a long, long time.

The country roads—none were then asphalted—were narrow and the many lanes were scarcely wide enough for an Army pick-up truck. Our slightly wider petrol-driven Bren gun carriers had great difficulty in negotiating them, yet they represented field and farm boundaries and when we knocked them down we were requested to kindly put them up again. Which we did as near as possible. Our live-and-let-live policy made movement that much more awkward but ensured friendly relations. Hitler himself was later to delay invasion and advise that the myriad of stone walls criss-crossing Malta could themselves defeat an airborne landing.

The people, who rose to such great heights of determination during the blitz and demonstrated so much stamina in the foodless, fuelless, homeless days showed great kindness towards us and most spoke some English. They were stocky, tanned and smiling and their Catholic religion took them to church daily, usually at four and five in the morning, and ensured that the young maidens were well chaperoned. If any soldier did speak to a girl he always found that at least one of her large number of brothers was there, too. Those who went home to tea entertained mother mostly, but dad, too, was interested and interesting. We soon learnt their normal philosophy of "Not to worry, Joe," a phrase we had not known before and which, although universally common today, I am perfectly certain originated in Malta.

Almost immediately we were to experience and enjoy the exuberance of the small boys of the families, at first shy but ever curious, willing to help until they became almost a nuisance, and certainly a worry when raids were on. In the shortage which gradually came upon us they demonstrated in their small way that inherited sense of business acumen that had enabled their forefathers to succeed as entrepreneurs through the centuries. Their forte was offering for sale back to tobacco-hungry soldiers those same cigarettes that they had freely given them in their generosity.

A feature of the times were the herds of goats kept for milk and cheese. They accompanied the 'milkman' around the villages to each door where every 'delivery' was guaranteed fresh and still warm. Soon they were to disappear and the people had to learn to use tinned cows' milk, of which they disapproved, not liking the taste. Later they perforce accepted dried milk and a nation's habits were changed.

Many of the country houses had a pair of animal horns attached to the roof. Like the upturned horseshoes nailed 'for good luck' to the doors of some older houses in England the horns were considered to be a beneficent influence. The use of both symbols might well have derived from the same period—the visits of the Romans over 2,000 years ago. When questioned about the horns the countryfolk, if they answered at all, would only intimate that they were there to ward off evil. They could have derived from the Romans' adoption of the Persian sun god Mithras, usually pictured in the act of slaying a bull.

But their usage as a talisman could have originated even earlier, influenced by the Phoenicians, who also visited Britain. Their chief goddess was Astarte, who ensured fertility and was sometimes represented as a cow. The moon was her emblem and the horns could well originally have had the double purpose of representing the crescent and the cow. We wondered where all these old sets of horns had come from as cattle were not tended on the island. However, whether Mithras or Astarte was responsible the horns were also demonstrated in a Maltese hand sign showing the first and little fingers upturned with the others curled. This was definitely a sign made to avert the evil eye but never openly, always behind the back—as a sort of very, very potent 'keeping the fingers crossed' of the Englishman.

Here we were in a country area among countryfolk. Later we would discover other strata of society including those keeping a stiff upper lip by continuing to attend concerts and other social gatherings organized by the British Institute. This was run by the British Council and did a good job—although some felt in a rather snooty or haughty fashion—by remaining open in Valletta and continuing to hold functions even in the craziest, noisiest days of blitz and bombardment. Some few people affected to ignore the bombing, but not many, and when a bomber made a black shadow between God and their own small patch of earth and the whistling sound began, each one rapidly remembered the simple principles of self-preservation. But this is digressing.

There was a night curfew from dusk to dawn. None needed it. Few desired to move around at night. It was always safer and wiser to be near the hole or shelter you knew. The military man on patrol or visiting detached posts on foot or by cycle soon learnt the sounds of the Malta night. There are no trains in Malta. There were then no ships to call, no docks lighted in welcome, no street lamps, no night buses. Just the blackout and the night. Yet it is easier to move around by the light of the stars than with the aid of a torch.

There were no disturbing man-made sounds as there are in peace—no distant clanking of milk churns, nor chugging of brewery engines, no slamming of car doors. Only the quiet of the countryside with the croaking of frogs, the rattle of beetles, the clop of a lone restless goat and the occasional braying of a donkey.

But the villages had their own sound. In Palestine one could smell a village before sighting it. In Malta a village could be heard. Yet 'heard' is too loud a word. As one approached one felt a quiet, satisfying murmur that flowed through the hot, still air like an echo in the mind. Into the night came the low mumbling of evening prayers and the telling of beads. Not from the basilica-like church whose great mass loomed high over the streets and the public square, but from within the homes. In the heat of a summer night windows would be open behind cooling shutters and many front doors would welcome any slight breeze.

From within and even from the doorsteps came the murmur of people at prayer. Thus, after the day's toil the village relaxed prepared for the night, thinking of the day past and the day to come. And the new day would begin with the dawn or pre-dawn visit to the church for early Mass.

Maltese families are usually large with six, seven or more children and there is a great sense of community. Relatives are counted in hundreds and a wedding reception is a most expensive business. Equally each death affects so very many intimately, a fact that gave to every casualty in war a very wide personal impact indeed. Also when you live on a tiny island each knows each, all know all, every face is familiar and it is impossible to be other than one family, one nation.

So friendliness and comradeship progressed, while the bombing continued and increased, especially on and around Grand Harbour, the submarine base at Manoel Island and the airfields at Luqa, Ta'Qali and Hal Far. It spread over into Valletta and the Three Cities, into Sliema and the country areas. The frequent stand-tos, the waiting, the crashes and roars, the harassment by the night bombers, were beginning to become monotonous, wearying and annoying.

Occasionally the Governor's daughter, Sybil Dobbie, would ride over from San Anton Palace to our San Loretto chapel area at the crack of cool dawn, around stand-to time, finding her way through the narrow lanes and picking a course between rubble, barbed wire and bomb holes. Not to visit us specifically but the area in general and particularly our pet gunners, being erstwhile horsemen, who had a post close by our D Company headquarters.

Horseriding at this early hour, just at the end of the night curfew, gave her some relaxation from the administrative work she was doing in the Governor's office, VAD nursing, Girl Guide supervising and the necessary all-embracing 'soldiers' welfare'. This ranged from procuring and supplying dart-boards for isolated posts to keeping men and wives in touch, sometimes a most difficult task when one was in war-battered, family-scattered Britain and the other in besieged, isolated Malta. Sybil recorded in *Grace Under Malta*, and I am grateful for the memory, how the countryfolk reacted to the rain of shell splinters that came pattering down after each gun opened fire. They would say "it is coming on to bomb" and take shelter in a doorway or under a lean-to while the 'shower' lasted.

DESPATCH TO ENGLAND

Continuing my journeying on this earth
I came upon an isle near Sicily,
A silver Island in an azure sea,
An Island, England, proudly bound to thee.

Across the vast expanse of ocean, free,
We rushed, my comrades and knew not the worth
Of this fair rock, nor how a humble mirth
Could keep alive a soul of royal birth.

Malta we found there silent, unafraid,
Ready and steady. Fitted to be made
The bride of destiny, the hope, the light
Of mankind struggling in the night.

And still she stands unbowed beneath the might
Of furious fiends; bleeding from the fight.
Yet let them pound and pound, that iron will
Has proved that David beats Goliath still.

FIVE

Heads Down — Hearts High

In isolated, besieged Malta the soldiers, sailors and airmen lived, worked and fought four-square with the civilian population. There were also, particularly among the airmen, Australians, New Zealanders, Rhodesians, Canadians and other Commonwealth servicemen playing their parts to keep Malta not only alive but aggressive. Aiding them, whenever they could get through, were the indomitable courageous seamen of the Merchant Navy, without whom the island and its people could not have succeeded nor, indeed, survived.

The Maltese have a special place in their hearts for these incredibly brave men who were sitting targets all the way, who knew the odds were against them getting through and who knew that two-thirds or more of their ships would almost certainly be sunk, their cargoes lost and their crews killed in every heroic effort to reach the island. Yet they still tried and tried again to bring sustenance to those in desperate need. The Maltese, in their own suffering, knew the perils the seamen endured and praised and respected them. There was never more satisfying a welcome for any tired, battered and bedraggled merchantman than the cheering crowds packing the battlements around Grand Harbour.

NO CHARGE FOR DELIVERY

You can sink yourself in wisdom, you can think you're
doing fine.
Have you ever had a thirst you couldn't slake?
Have you ever seen a convoy with the good ships there in
line
And the bullets singing, stinging in the wake?

Have you ever seen torpedoes dashing straight across your
bows
As you slew the ship around and miss 'em fine?
Have you ever seen fat bombers screaming down like ugly
sows
And the ships a-slick and steady in their line?

Have you ever seen the packets from the bombers as they
                                                    drop?

Have you ever felt them as they crack the deck?
Have you ever felt the choking when your eyeballs nearly
                                                    pop

As the blast comes back and almost breaks your neck?

Have you ever seen a seaman lying dead across his gun
With the flames a-licking round him bit by bit?
Have you ever seen the bodies burning when the ship is
                                                    done?

If you had you wouldn't ever lose your kit.

Have you ever seen the blood and sweat that thousands
                                            pay in kind

To bring the stuff you're wasting day by day?
Have you ever seen the telegrams to those they left behind,
The charge for which is *not* against your pay?

Have you ever seen . . . well have you? 'Course you have
                                            and quite a bit.
Can you see the stuff they're piling on the quay?
Can you see the price that's written? P'raps you can't
                                            decipher it.
It was paid for twice, thrice over as they brought it through
                                            the sea.

Of course, it was the Royal Navy that helped, guarded and
shepherded the merchantmen through. Force K of two
cruisers and two destroyers did a remarkable job but not
merely as defensive guardians. Their aggressive sorties resulting in dare-devil successes were an inspiration to the people
of Malta, proving that the Axis was not unbeatable and that
determination, enterprise and daring paid dividends. Their
example helped the islanders to endure.

Force K was supplemented from time to time as Admiral
Cunningham was able, or found it advisable, to move warships from other areas. For instance, the 14th Destroyer
Flotilla was sent to Malta from the Aegean in early April
1941 to harass Axis convoys and fared magnificently. Led by

H.M.S. *Jervis*, the vessels were *Janus*, *Nubian* and *Mohawk*. They were later joined by the cruiser *Gloucester*. In May 1941 Captain Lord Louis Mountbatten in the cruiser *Kelly* was similarly detached to operate from Malta against enemy convoys with the 5th Destroyer Flotilla, whose vessels were *Kashmir*, *Kelvin*, *Kipling* and *Jackal*.

Let two naval actions speak for the aggressive, daring and highly successful warships operating from Malta and of their striking power. On 15 April 1941 the 14th Destroyer Flotilla sped out of Grand Harbour to intercept an enemy convoy spotted by a Swordfish reconnaissance plane. They found the convoy in the early hours and in an intense and well organized action that Captain Mack, commanding *Jervis*, modestly described as "the skirmish off Sfax", they destroyed the five merchantmen and their escort of three destroyers. H.M.S. *Mohawk* was sunk but her captain and crew, singing lustily "Roll Out The Barrel", were picked up by *Jervis* and *Nubian*, guided by the choruses.

On 8 November 1941 Force K, commanded by Captain W. G. Agnew, and consisting of the cruisers *Aurora* and *Penelope* and the destroyers *Lively* and *Lance*, left Malta at high speed for the toe of Italy where a reconnaissance plane had sighted a convoy of ten merchantmen off Cape Spartivento. Just after midnight the convoy was located escorted by four destroyers. With pre-arranged co-ordinated attack drill Force K disposed of two destroyers, while the other two fled. Force K then discovered another two large ships escorted by two more destroyers. They disposed of the merchant vessels in the first convoy one by one and then engaged the last two destroyers which also turned tail to escape. The submarine *Upholder* came upon the scene, identified herself, and set course for the burning vessels still afloat, while Force K returned to Malta. *Upholder* torpedoed and sank two more destroyers to bring the total 'bag' for the night to ten merchant ships destroyed and four destroyers sunk.

Such daring and determined actions resulting in huge enemy losses were proof and typical of Malta's aggressive capabilities and caused the enemy of necessity to increase his escorts. It also made this scorpion of an island even more the centre point for aerial attention and obliteration, but such positive results from determined action also boosted the people's morale.

So Malta presented a completely stubborn and co-ordinated front to the enemy. The gunners and airmen worked out routines to cope jointly with enemy air attacks. The infantry guarded, defended, built and repaired the airfields and the splinter-proof aircraft pens: The Queen's Own Royal West Kents and the Buffs at Luqa, the Manchesters at Ta'Qali, the Devonshires at Hal Far Royal Navy airfield, the King's Own Malta Regiment at Hal Far and Qrendi, and the Hampshires with a small detachment for a time at Qrendi and for some time at Hal Far, but mostly making, extending and defending the new strip at Safi, which adjoined Luqa and was part of a scheme to link up with Hal Far. Before Qrendi airfield was built I was assigned the task to site defensive positions and then with a detachment of platoon strength from D Company of the Hampshires had for a short time the task of defending it. This was a most vulnerable area situated at the head of three *wieds* which ran down through high cliffs to the rocky coast. Enemy planes could approach low over the sea and swoop up through the most southerly *wieds* with surprising suddenness. In the evening the glare of the declining sun, almost blinding the eyes of our Bren gunners, made the westerly *wied* the best approach route, while the high cliffs stretching south-eastward from Dingli deadened the sound of approaching marauders who could again come in unseen and unheard until the last vital seconds. Nevertheless, the airfield was built and the King's Own Malta Regiment took on the task of defending it.

The Malta Police worked at Safi in the early stages, and the Malta Pioneer Group, formed in 1942, helped fill in the bomb holes and built pens at Luqa and Ta'Qali with earth-filled petrol tins and blocks of limestone. The Pioneers were of great assistance to the Royal Engineers. No. 2601 Company of the Malta Pioneer Group under Major 'Smokey' Donaldson organized immense smoke screens around the Grand Harbour and Marsamxett, a defensive effort that was most effective but also often disconcerting, to say the least, to the people on the ground. The sappers, concerned with defence works, also did much tunnelling to preserve in underground chambers the small amount of rainwater that annually falls on the island. Water, one of the main essentials of life, was necessarily rationed. Officially at nine gallons per head — about a third of the usual requirement in England — it amounted to much less in some areas with taps turned off for long hours each day. In some districts, where mains were opened by bombing, water was delivered by cart — resulting in more time- and energy-consuming queues. In the hot weather and in overcrowded conditions this was just another hardship, especially as the beaches were no longer available. Even if they had been, travel to them was difficult and exposure in any numbers would only have invited Messerschmitt cannon and machine-gun fire.

All regiments helped to fill in the bomb craters on the airfields immediately they were made. This was a daily, hour after hour, necessary task at the height of the blitz and, in spite of the immense risks, troops did not wait for the all-clear. Our planes depended on safe landing areas and airborne fighters were a necessary means of defence. The troops also learned to become expert in refuelling and rearming the planes in such extremely quick time that their wait on the ground during an air alert was cut down to a matter of a few minutes. Also, the anti-aircraft gunners maintained a circle of guns that ensured a safety orbiting zone for incoming planes unable to land, where they could circle at low altitude. Here, while they were waiting to land, fighters which had used up their ammunition were comparatively safe from the ever-active Luftwaffe.

AWAITING BATTLE

Fear not for me my Dear, my faithful Heart,
Lest I should fail in thinking of your fear;
A soldier must be wedded to his art
And let no call but honour hold him dear.

So let me stand on this fair British rock
And let my eye be true, my aim be straight;
And should the Hun set foot and live to mock,
Trust God Who knows my fate.

For we will stand while yet a British heart
Beats on this soil; while yet we've breath to give.
Tell them at home, if death should be our part,
We die that England live.

The 10,500 dockyard workers, including the strong-backed
stevedores, played an heroic part, being subject to danger all
through their working day. They had difficulties in getting to
work as bus routes were curtailed and there were no buses on
Saturdays and Sundays. Their normal weekly forty-seven
hours were perforce worked during the remaining five days
of the week, extending each working day to nine or ten
hours, even without overtime. This naturally tried their
strength, already feeling the effects of the meagre rations.
Many wives went short of food that their men might retain
sufficient strength to continue the hard work in the dockyard.
Some paid as much as 2*s*. 6*d*. for the occasional egg to aid
existence.

Before the war farm workers and labourers, such as
stevedores with high energy-expending tasks, ate little meat
but about six pounds of bread a day. Many would scoop the
centre from a loaf, insert goat or sheep cheese, tomatoes or
lettuce, and enjoy a good meal. Now they were reduced to
three-quarters of a pound of bread and perhaps a portion of
bully beef. A loaf of bread, if obtainable, could cost up to 10
shillings. To augment the stevedores the troops also helped to
unload quickly any ship that did come in.

The gunners, Royal Artillery and Royal Malta Artillery,
were magnificent. Under the energetic Major-General C. T.
Beckett, who commanded the Artillery of the Fortress from
May 1941 to December 1942, they played a full, heroic,
meritorious part against almost impossible odds. They
worked their guns until they were red hot, the barrels wore
out and ammunition ran short, but they never faltered nor
failed. Their splendid barrage over the harbours with tracer
interlaced exceeded any spectacle that could be imagined,
and scored fine successes. It seemed impossible for any plane
to live within it and few chanced it. Yet Stuka dive bombers
did get through though many perished in the attempt.

The daring, darting Spitfires—when they did eventually
arrive—followed the enemy into this holocaust, showing

courage that will long be remembered by Maltese and British alike. At night the spectacle was even more brilliant with the Bofors' red shot intermingling with other tracer, while searchlights sought and held the enemy intruders. There came a time when, if a bombing raid was obviously pin-pointed to one area, hundreds, maybe thousands, of people would watch from flat rooftops and applaud the prowess of brave men, quite forgetting that they were in a world apart and could never hear the plaudits.

Nevertheless, ammunition was precious and as time went on and the siege tightened barrages were normally reserved for large plots of enemy aircraft—100, perhaps 250 or 300 or more at a time. Then at night the policy would sometimes be 'Douse!' when not a speck of light could be seen. During air raids all troops would be standing by and the civilians would be alert, too. Then the man in the slit trench, the sentry on a tower, the priest in his steeple, the gunner by a Bofors, and the housewife sitting just within her open front door because the heat of a summer night made the air in the shelter too stifling, then all these would be holding their breath expectantly, trying to recognize the sound of the engines. Theirs or ours? Junkers or Wellingtons, Messerschmitts or Hurricanes, Swordfish, Beauforts, Beaufighters? The atmosphere would be tense, no movement, nothing to show that thousands were listening and waiting.

Sometimes a marauder would fly round and round seeking a target at a steady engine pace, then would come a quickening and a louder roar as the plane swooped on its bombing run, then an infinitesimal pause while it lifted as the bomb fell away and then the smack and explosion of the missile. Sometimes there would be no bomb, but the waiting and expectancy would always be there. Like waiting for that second shoe to drop when the man in the flat above goes to bed—but this was a one-legged man with an assassin's explosive devilry. Sometimes low cloud would deceive the pilot and the circling would recede until the lost plane was many miles from Malta's shores. Always the island would be alert and that sense of watching wakefulness became a way of life.

SUNSET OVER MALTA

There in the gloom a woman's quiet sighs,
And here beneath the bough a sparrow's cheep.
A farmer wending homeward notes the skies
And thinks upon tomorrow and his sheep.

A herd of goats go clip-clop through the lane
As barefoot Zeppu leads them to their shed.
He stops beside the shrine, but with disdain
The goats move on intent on food and bed.

A sailor in his white loose-fitting suit
Remains a while and leans upon the wall.
While there towards the sunset with his flute
A budding minstrel trills his evening call.

The setting sun in rich and royal red
Now quickly sinks behind Mdina's towers.
The world stands hushed, while from her daytime bed
The night bat stirs, prepared for her short hours.

A pair of lovers move beneath the trees,
Their fingers touching lightly. Now the shrouds
Of night descend and with the cooling breeze
Comes from afar the murmuring of the crowds.

The laughter of the children in the streets,
The merriment of rest from daily toil,
The murmur of the evening prayers, the sweets
Of home life after wrestling with the soil.

And here the nightly watch has just begun,
The sentry passing slowly on his way.
The searchlight crews and gunners one by one
Go to their well-known posts and wait the day.

And on the dromes are pilots standing by;
And on the beaches all defences manned.
A quiet throbbing in the distant sky.
A waiting silence overcomes the land.

The Royal Corps of Signals had a difficult task to keep communications effective, especially the telephones—the lines being so often blasted out by bombing. They also helped to keep in working order the island's Rediffusion system of relaying news, entertainment, announcements and air-raid warnings by landline. Regimental signallers were fully employed and coped valiantly in their own areas, often having to go out several times a day and by night to repair and replace lines damaged and destroyed by bombs.

The infantry in the field, tactically deployed against air and sea attacks and in defending important posts and vulnerable areas, such as airfields, aircraft pens, dispersal points and communicating access lanes, were continuously on alert. Their chief defence weapons were the Bren gun and twin Lewis guns mounted offensively against aircraft. Of no use against high-level heavy bombers, this small arms fire could yet be lethal to Stuka dive-bombers. But if the planes were coming straight for the gun the chances were approximately the same if the gunner hit or not—obliteration by bomb or crashing plane. The Bren and Lewis could also effectively engage the Messerschmitt wall-hopping cannon-firing marauder; but the chances were heavily against any infantry success as the planes roared in suddenly only thirty or forty feet above ground, spattering the area with cannon and machine-gun fire, and were gone in barely a second.

Most posts experienced the trauma of delayed-action bombs planted around them and had, in consequence, to move from time to time. Many, especially those by *wieds* near the coast, were the objectives of wall-hopping intruders. One Hampshire position, commanded by Sergeant Harry Bowers, had a metal object flung at it by a low-flying plane. "What secret weapon now?" thought the sergeant. When it was eventually gathered in it was seen to be a large, heavy, aircraft spanner, but this was not a chance discard for written across it was the intended intimidatory wishful-thinking message: MALTA ITALIANO.

The infantry did bring down planes when luck and the intense courage of Bren or Lewis gunner got a good sight in time and hung on doggedly to put a full magazine of lead into the intruder. There were crashed planes and pieces of

planes interspersing the bomb craters all around the countryside, some our own. Many British and Commonwealth pilots
owe their lives to infantrymen who rushed to their rescue
when they crash-landed and extricated them before the plane
blew up. Some rescuers were rewarded for their heroism and
well they deserved it; many faded into the background and
oblivion when the immediate urgent task was done. It was all
part of life by day and by night in a continuous comradely
team effort to survive and overcome.

The Governor was Commander in Chief of all forces and
under him the General Officer Commanding was responsible
for the efficiency of the troops. Major General D. M. W.
Beak, VC, was what the Americans would call 'a hot
cookie' — the British troops used another phrase. Unlike many
generals of World War One he was personally known to the
troops and made his presence felt. He arrived on the island in
January 1942 and obviously intended to keep the troops on
their toes. There was real chance of an invasion and he was
there with the task of getting the garrison ready to repel it.
The shortage of food was already being felt, but the men had
to be thoroughly fit, agile and fully conversant with their task
should raiders attempt to breach the shore defences or
descend from the skies.

Physical training for all ranks and all ages became regular
routine and there were 'mobility marches' which entailed fast
movement from point to point, including running in battle
kit for part of each hour. All this in addition to the other
strenuous tasks the PBI were tackling. We soon knew the
terrain thoroughly, including those places where parachute
troops could possibly land — much of the countryside was too
difficult for them, being divided into small fields, all
boundaried by dry-stone walls and interspersed by deep
quarries. Possible landing sites were safeguarded by erecting
poles at intervals. They cast little shadow, could hardly be
seen from the air, yet could have overturned planes or gliders
and disrupted landings.

The Hampshires were used to this kind of intensive
mobility training and took it in their stride. We had known a
commanding officer of like calibre in India — Lieutenant
Colonel W. H. Ramsden, who later as a major-general
clashed with Montgomery on handing over 8th Army to him

at Alamein. They were of like temperament and determination, able to steer a clear path through a mass of irrelevancies and intent on carrying a job through to its vital conclusion. The Hampshires had also served under Montgomery in Palestine, so General Beak's tough training was tackled without tantrums. Any resentment disappeared when his official residence in Valletta was bombed. To the troops he had minimized the power of the bombing, saying soon after his arrival from England, or so it was reported and flashed round the garrison: "You don't know what bombing is!" As he had just come in from blitzed Britain, we understood the viewpoint but not the method of presentation. Others had misinterpreted a lull; we knew he would soon be fully informed—by the Boche. He was. A bomb, apparently actually aimed at his be-flagged residence, cleanly cut out his lavatory but did not explode—just after he had left it, so they said. Who knows? Of such things are legends built. There were many tales of humorous narrow escapes in blitzed Malta, including one of a man who was still sitting on his throne when the side of his house was sliced away. True or not, there was a lavatory pan complete with seat and cistern high on a wall in Valletta for many months. It must have taken great ingenuity to rescue the incumbent if the tale was true.

General Beak left the island in August, after staying only just over six months, to shake up some other poor beggars, we thought, now the threat of invasion had receded. He left behind a garrison in a high state of fitness, ready and waiting, and in a way irritated at not being able to get at the enemy. Major-General R. MacK. Scobie, who took his place, still required a first-class efficiency, absolute alertness and readiness for action, whatever, wherever and whenever it might be. He also allowed some easement in set parades. The food shortage was striking harder now and there was also much strenuous work being undertaken by the infantry on airfields and at times in the harbour area.

Later, in Cairo on 12 February 1943, General Scobie was to tell war correspondents: "One reason the Germans were unable to take Malta was that they never had sufficient parachute troops and aircraft available at the right time." But, he believed, they were still bound to try to "have a smack at

Malta when and if they evacuate Tunisia". We know now that they were never able to evacuate — the Axis lost nearly 300,000 men there taken as prisoners. We also know that the crucial date was already past. It was in the month of June 1942 — during General Beak's watchful sojourn on the island. Then the Germans were ready to 'take out' Malta but Rommel was keener to chase 8th Army pulling away to the east and to destroy the Desert Rats in the field before they could reach safety in Egypt. Also before his own lines of communication had become too extended.

Tobruk fell on 21 June. That same day Kesselring flew in to the battered fortress where he met Rommel and reminded him that the Luftwaffe air squadrons would now concentrate again on Malta. Rommel, exuberant with success, was certain that he could catch and defeat 8th Army and force a way right through to the Suez Canal. Tobruk would give him the forward harbour he needed for his fuel supplies. He intended to press on. All this in spite of Mussolini's directive in May that he should halt at the Egyptian frontier to allow Malta to be 'taken out' and the menace to the Italian navy and convoys removed. Kesselring, although keen to annihilate Malta, eventually agreed with Rommel and promised to ensure supplies. Meanwhile, in Germany the Chief of the Armed Forces Planning Staff said: "We have Tobruk, we do not need Malta." On this same day, 21 June, Hitler was once again questioned about implementing Operation Herkules — the German–Italian invasion of Malta — and still wavered. He said the British were falling back on all fronts — the Russians, too — and there was no need yet to take Malta. He backed Rommel's impulse and so informed Mussolini. In the event Rommel lost Montgomery and Kesselring lost Malta.

Scobie told the correspondents that the infantry garrisoning Malta also patrolled ninety miles of beaches and rocky coastline and that during the heavy bombing soldiers helped to unload convoys at night, working a system of twelve hours on and twelve hours off duty. With regard to the island's "great feat of endurance", he said that in August 1942 it was certain that if relief did not come by mid-November the people would have starved within a few weeks. He said there were three reasons for Malta's survival: the houses being made of stone did not burn; there were deep shelters; and the morale of the population was always high, the people being tough and prepared to put up with a surprising degree of privation. He paid tribute to the Royal Air Force and the gunners who "did magnificently" and declared that "very great credit" must be given to the infantry for the considerable amount of work they had done, including great assistance to the Royal Air Force in servicing machines, filling in craters and building several hundred huge pens for harbouring aircraft. The infantry, he said, were looking forward to the time when they could take a more active part in warlike operations.

Indeed they were and some, the Malta Brigade, would in the not too distant future land with Montomery in Sicily, chase the Boche in Italy, take their place in the D-Day Normandy landings in the first wave and in the traditional place of honour on the extreme right of the line and continue chasing across Europe.

By a coincidence the morning that General Scobie's observations were reported in a Reuter message in the *Times of Malta*, the newspaper also published a Maltese reader's letter which suggested: "that the Garrison of Malta who stood up so bravely and hit back so hard at the Huns and Wops be granted some sort of badge or insignia such as a Maltese Cross . . . surmounted by the word 'Malta' and with the letters 'G C' one on either side of the cross, as a recognition of the great service they have rendered the Empire here in Malta".

Also in this edition — and I mention it to show that the war, the siege and privation were still very much with us in 1943 — was a public notice declaring that a very limited number of eggs were available and would be distributed through chemists at 1s. 2d. each. (A high price, but very much lower than the Black Market.) They would be issued for children "up to two years of age", with the proviso that "in the case of very young infants the eggs will, of course, be for the benefit of the nursing mother". There would also be some available for sufferers from Diabetes mellitus "on production of a medical certificate".

But let us still remember the time of high blitz and powerful bombing. When the tempo of bombing increased so did the enemy casualties. During the siege the guns and air-craft of Malta brought down 1,129 enemy aircraft, of which the guns claimed 236. The island lost 568 planes.

SIX

Death at Dawn

The only seaborne attack on Malta came in with the dawn on 26 July 1941. The episode began in anticipatory and tensely dramatic silence with the coastal gunners of the Royal Malta Artillery waiting through the long night with itching 'trigger fingers' for the attack to come in and it ended with much of the population of Valletta standing on rooftops and other vantage points to watch a devastating display of pyrotechnics directed seawards. All backed by the booming of coastal guns — an angry roaring sound not heard before.

The Royal Malta Artillery were the regular soldiers of the island with a long ancestry and for a year now they had been manning the coastal defences — as well as anti-aircraft guns — perfecting their techniques, co-ordinating their intricate criss-cross firing lines and waiting patiently while they wondered when, and if ever, they would be needed in earnest. As the siege tightened and Mussolini and Hitler made more and more threatening noises, and as the bombing intensified, all began to feel that a full invasion attempt must be made at some time. So when during the night of 25–26 July the Italian warship *Diana* was detected by Royal Air Force radar to be stationary about nine miles offshore, the coastal batteries were alerted. The reason for the warship's positioning was not understood. It might have been for laying mines or as a decoy for enticement but the long stay was certainly suspicious. It might have been the rendezvous point for something bigger. In any case a convoy had only just reached Malta and was now safely in Grand Harbour and the cargo was precious.

The civilian population had answered the air-raid siren early that night and had taken their precautions, some as usual going to the shelters, some waiting in their homes in case it was merely a nuisance raid, and there had been no bombing. It was just an eerie long wait through the dark hours with some feeling of wondering anxiety — although the populace knew nothing of the warship. Some of the gunners, although they knew so very little more, decided to wait right beside their guns. Their commanders knew about the warship and there was just a chance that the coastal defences might this night be needed and could at last prove their worth. They had waited through long months and knew of the denigrating insults and bombastic threats repeatedly made by Rome Radio.

There had been long night alerts before but this did not lull the sentries into carelessness. Not only were they looking skywards but the coast defence gunners, especially those at Forts St Elmo, Ricasoli and Tigne, were keenly trying to pierce the night gloom to watch the sea. Also waiting and watchful were the machine-gunners of the Cheshire Regiment and the Lancashire Fusiliers positioned around the harbours. If anything got through the boom supporting the submarine net that closed the entrance it would stand little chance against these experts, some of whom I had already seen in action when I had a section temporarily within my command in the Western Dessert.

Meanwhile, aboard the *Diana* preparations were being made for an attack on the shipping the Italians knew to be in Grand Harbour and also on the submarine base in Marsamxett, another large harbour (*Marsa* means harbour) on the northern side of Valletta. About eighteen swift-moving powerful craft were assembled ready for the attempt which had been well rehearsed by men who knew that this was indeed a dangerous mission in which they might well forfeit their lives. Apart from their expertise in handling each craft and its missiles, and in getting clear from the vessels at the precise instant, their one hope of success was surprise and, therefore, remaining undetected until the last possible moment.

In the event, the defence was waiting, though they knew not what to expect, but the boats were so low in the water that they came in under the island's defensive radar screen. They were close inshore, coming at a rattling pace through the grey-green gloom of the early morning when all the defenders could hear was the throb of powerful engines. Some of these vessels were E-boats: fast, big, motor launches with powerful engines and carrying torpedoes. They were a type already familiar to both the Axis and the Allies and were difficult to combat successfully. There was also a new type of one-man torpedo boat, a secret weapon invented by the Italians and of which they were intensely proud. They claimed to have tried it out by attacking the Gibraltar defences before the Malta attempt and the leader at Malta had gained experience on that earlier raid. His craft was probably blasted out of the water during the run in to the Grand Harbour for his body was never found.

These secret one-man craft were highly dangerous to handle in action and almost certain to cause destruction. They were small boats with the bow tightly packed with high explosives. There was an engine amidships and just enough room for the pilot to crouch in the tiny stern. He wore an immersion suit and the theory was that he should aim the craft at the objective, pull a lever to activate the charge, then abandon ship. The craft would continue on its way and explode on impact. If he was lucky the pilot would be picked up by an E-boat after it, too, had cast its torpedoes.

In training, drills can be perfected and difficulties over-come. In action there is another element — the opposition. At Malta the opposition was waiting. They had waited all night, though they knew not for what. When the throb of engines was heard out at sea the defenders were still in doubt as to the nature of the attack but they, too, had drilled and trained to attain perfection. Now they waited just that little bit longer until the new menace, whatever it was, had almost reached the shore.

The Italians, speeding towards the coast without apparent opposition from what they had been told was an extremely well defended fortress, were priding themselves on achieving surprise. Then suddenly a mass of searchlights opened up at sea level, illuminating them all, and the guns immediately brought down a devastating fire which the ratatat of machine guns and the interweaving red and white tracer developed into a dramatic curtain of death. It was all over in six minutes and none escaped. One boat exploded at the boom and another at the adjacent viaduct. There were a few prisoners, one wounded at the viaduct and two taken further along the coast at St George's Bay, having missed Valletta's harbours by more than two miles. All others perished. The *Diana* waited but none returned. An aerial bombardment by planes stationed in Sicily, which should have synchronized with the seaborne approach, never came in. Maybe this was fortunate for the defenders but it would have made no difference to the outcome as the attackers had lost the one element, surprise, that might have gained them the chance of some success.

As the dawn broke Hurricanes took off and searched the sea, found two craft, sank one and killed the occupants of the other. They set out to find the *Diana* and discovered her sailing fast back to Augusta in Sicily, escorted by a screen of Macchi fighters. In the air scrap that ensued at least five Macchis were shot down and two Hurricanes were lost, the pilot of one baling out into the sea. He managed to scramble aboard the still floating E-boat full of dead Italians. In the heat and hurry of battle he might easily have been mistakenly machine-gunned as an enemy, but luckily he was spotted and identified by a Swordfish floatplane which rescued him. He took with him the E-boat's flag which became a treasured trophy for his squadron.

What of the civilian population? After an all-night alert some were in the shelters, other fitfully sleeping in their homes, but when they heard the boom of the coastal guns, for the first time in the war, they knew that the menace was from the sea. With no bombs falling they felt safe to leave their houses and shelters and to seek vantage points on rooftops and bastions. No doubt in 1565 the much smaller population had watched in some such like manner when the Turks invaded those three centuries earlier, before the city of Valletta with its vast fortifications was built. For all they knew now this was another invasion, yet they did not run, they went to watch. Others a little further inland also heard the guns, the explosions and the chatter and clatter of machine-gun fire. They could not see and as rumour chased rumour there was for a while a real belief that the invasion so many had expected had really begun. Fortunately there was no panic nor precipitant movement of the inhabitants and soon the truth became known and fears allayed.

This action was a setback for the Italian secret weapon which had achieved so little and had not penetrated any Malta defence. The crew of the *Diana* was dejected at the failure and their attitude had a demoralizing effect within the Italian navy. Rome Radio still claimed a success saying that nine torpedoes had been carried, nine had been fired, and nine explosions were heard aboard *Diana*. The announcer said "This proves the success of our enterprise." Quite ignoring the possibility that the explosions came from the craft as they were hit going in. The announcement may have deceived the Italians but not the Maltese who knew well the distortions, inaccuracies and downright lies broadcast from Rome. Once had they not claimed to have sunk H.M.S. *St Angelo* in Grand Harbour? This 'warship', the head-quarters of the Vice Admiral Malta, was and still is a 'stone frigate' built as a fort by the Knights. The Maltese never believed anything out of Rome — although the world might.

For the Maltese the outcome of this the only seaborne attack was a fine morale booster. They had proved their training and their defences and they had proved, too, that they could defeat surprise by surprise. For they had waited tensely and without any inadvertent action until the last possible moment before opening fire. Waited until they could almost 'see the whites of their eyes', as the English infantry squares had done in ages past.

This was a classic action — a fine example of preparedness and then concentration of effort at the vital moment. A display of discipline that ensured the defenders fired not one single shot, nor Very light, nor star shell to signify their awareness. Radar was in its infancy and the Italians might not have been aware that *Diana* could be detected at the long range of nine miles. The attackers certainly thought they had surprise, but it was they who were surprised in the end. During war, battles often take a long time to build up but the actual action is frequently short. Then training, discipline, concentration, example and courage count. This, the only seaborne attack on Malta in World War Two, will be long remembered. Like the siege of Malta itself it is the stuff of which legends are made.

The Chief of the Imperial General Staff at the War Office in London was among the first to send a congratulatory signal to the victorious defenders. He said:

Please convey my congratulations to all ranks of the Royal Malta Artillery manning fixed defences on their great success on breaking up the determined enemy seaborne attack on the Grand Harbour. The action of these gunners has excited universal admiration here in the United Kingdom. The skill and determination shown by them will act as a strong deterrent to future enemy attacks by sea.

The Secretary of State for the Colonies signalled the Governor:

I have learnt with much pleasure of the prominent part played by Maltese troops in the utter defeat of the recent Italian attack on Valletta harbour. They are to be congratulated on a splendid performance of which they and the people of Malta may justly be proud.

There was no further attempt by the Axis at this kind of 'surprise' raid, nor indeed of any seaborne landing or bombardment: but two-man 'baby' craft, carried by a 'mother' submarine, did go to the harbours of Gibraltar, Alexandria and Algiers where they penetrated the defences with devastating success. The Italians never dared again at Malta where the welcome that still awaited them would have been equally as warm and generous as on their first visit.

STAND TO!

Let the Boche come! Whatever may befall
We shall stand firm nor fail at Freedom's call.
Gird up your loins! Though blackest night begin,
Let the Boche come! *We will not let him in!*

Thought you his *kultur* better than our own?
Look at our hearths, our churches and our stone.
Heap upon heap—his method to enchain
The unfettered nations to his damnèd train.

Fear not the blows. We lose our kith and kin
But not our heart. *We will not let him in!*
Stand to your stations! Know your destined part.
The scum of nations cannot break our heart.

This is our day! Stand up and face the foe!
We cannot fail. Trust God, whose love we know.
Death and despoil may seem a bitter price —
There's one more cast: our firm hand holds the dice.

Stand to your posts! Be steadfast, bold of heart!
Each to his task, to each his practised part.
For Freedom! For our souls! Our hearth! Our kin!
Though death our part *we will not let him in!*

But the island's fight for survival was desperate. The Luftwaffe pounded and pounded with high-explosive bombs, incendiaries, landmines, cannon and machine-gun fire, sinking ships in harbour, destroying dock installations and mains services, laying mines to seaward and sometimes dropping the huge destructors on land, devastating the airfields, dive-bombing and flying in low to house-top and machine-gun at will. Eventually the villages were battered in preparation for the final assault before invasion that appeared to be a certainty.

The blitzing of the villages was a vicious procedure. At Mqabba the horrifying raid took a quarter of an hour and the bombers came in at lunchtime on 9 April 1942. No one expected a direct attack on tiny villages where life was concerned merely with the produce of the fields and was centred on the village church. Each village has its own distinctive church of cathedral proportions in which there is great pride.

When the bombers came to Mqabba many of the countryfolk had already answered the siren and were in the shelter but some sick and elderly and a few others were still in their homes. The doctor and the Protection Officer were standing alone in a small room ready to cope with injuries and rehousing but none expected the fury of direct bombing. Those tiny, narrow streets were no place to be in when it came, and when the last few realized the savagery of the attack and made a dash for the shelter, not all reached sanctuary. Their war ended then amid chaos and smoke haze and as they lay they were covered in fine yellow limestone powder and sickly grey bomb-dust. A stretcher party from the nearby D Company of the Hampshire Regiment rushed into the streets but there was nothing they could do. There were no injured lying there—only corpses, partly stripped by the bomb blast.

As the buildings rocked and the stonework fell, the people in the shelter were reciting the rosary and the air outside was a vast cloud of suffocating dust mixed with the smell of cordite, some of which blasted its way below. That is why shelters often had a pail of water just inside the entrance where a mother could dip a handkerchief and then cover a baby's nostrils against the contaminated air.

The parish priest was in the church tower when the bombers struck. They came at a quarter to one and were gone at one. A bomb went straight through the church. The clock tower remained standing but the church was an empty shell. The clock died at exactly 1 p.m. By a miracle the priest lived and walked down to comfort his flock.

MQABBA—NAZI QUARTER OF AN HOUR

A quarter to one; you can hear the clock chime.
We're proud of the clock and we love the old church.
It is glorious spring and we look at the time
Though the weird banshee wails and we hear the Hun
search.

The drone of the planes and the rushing of wind!
The thunder! The lightning! The tall buildings lurch.
Bomb dust and bricks! (O God, have we sinned?)
The debris, the craters, the hole in the church.

The ruin of homes, the stone and the dead.
The paintings of saints and the priest in his frock.
The clock tower intact, though its heart must have bled,
For its pulse beats no more, and it stares—one o'clock!

Meanwhile, in Sicily Royal Air Force reconnaissance planes had discovered glider fields and railheads being made ready for the assembly of what could only be an invading force on Malta. It seemed to be but a matter of time before the island's garrison and the island's people would be put to the supreme test.

INTO BATTLE

Now show the embittered foe the British race
Can give the blows we've taken and can face
The ravager of Europe under all
The trials of battle and can force the pace.

Now let the bastions and positions ring
Aloud with popping lead, the bullets sing.
Now let him bring his numbers and his best;
We'll prove once more this scorpion still can sting.

This scorpion, this Malta, in her side
In these past months has felt a wound undried;
Has taken blows, has reeled, nor found her rest,
Her houses down, and yet she has not died.

Not died? Not died! And nowhere near the brink.
The Boche will ponder if he can but think;
With thought enough he well may yet draw back
And purchase wisdom ere his forces sink.

But let him come! We wait him on the beach;
The air is ours, the fields, the dromes; no breach
Will he find here. No Trojan horse can draw
Unto these shores, nor traitor utter speech.

Now let our sky be grey with Nazi fools.
Who dares to strike us now we have the tools?
Up lads! The Boche is mad again today,
He lusts for power and soon forgets the rules.

Hold to your posts! Let not excursions blast
Your hopes, nor let your spirit be downcast.
To those of us who die, this epitaph:
"The flag still flies, they *nailed* it to the mast!"

SEVEN

Blazing Blitz

The towns and villages lay much in ruins. The heavy limestone blocks of which the houses were constructed were vast heaps of rubble. Whole streets were blocked and areas cut off. Churches, farmhouses, convents and palaces were not spared. The people lived in catacombs, caves, family-made holes hacked in the rocks and underground shelters. They hung their washing from trees, preparing their meals on the sidewalks, sleeping where they could and when they could under the constant raids. The bombers and fighters interrupted meals as well as sleep and the alerts and bombings often lasted throughout the night. Four raids in twenty-four hours could mean ten to twenty hours under alert. And this went on day after day, night after night.

Yet there were many who slept at home, fitfully perhaps, like cats with ears alert and senses tensed ready to move quickly to the shelters. In the hot summer some of these could be stifling. The winter of 1941–42 was the coldest and wettest for many years. They called it the 'Black Winter', for even the elements added agony to the hunger, the sleeplessness, the terror and the destruction. At least the rain eased the water supply, but it was cold then in the damp, underground holes and again many stayed at home. But 'home' was often open to the wind and rain with a room blasted out or a wall shored up and the way in was across a heap of rubble.

MOTHER MALTA

Oh the ruined towns of Malta
And the houses falling down,
And the stone upon the roadway,
And the white road turning brown,
And the blue distempered bedrooms
Laying stark unto the sun.
Oh the ruined towns of Malta,
They are heroes, every one.

See them standing in their splendour
As the sun dips in the west.
See the farmer wending slowly
To his home and food and rest.
Though there's precious little for him,
Malta, Mother, you are free,
And whatever else betide him
There is love and God and thee.

There is rubble on your mantle,
There is bomb-dust in your hair.
Oh your 'scutcheon should be rubble
With your cross resplendent there,
Held aloft by gay defenders,
Knights, civilians, charioteers,
Noble mariners encircling,
Like the old-time musketeers.

Oh the ruined towns of Malta,
And the houses falling down,
And the stone upon the roadway,
And the white road turning brown.
We shall leave you, Mother Malta,
Moving home across the sea,
Echoing still your battle challenge: ·
"Ye shall long remember me!"

As the siege tightened the gunners were limited to a few rounds a day and there were set hours for action. Yet the island's spirit of stubbornness showed in rigid discipline, even in its adherence to duty. "Why didn't you fire?" I asked a Royal Artillery sergeant in charge of a Bofors gun between Mqabba and Zurrieq when one evening a Messerschmitt came screaming in from the sea at housetop height, cannons chattering, bullets spattering. The Bofors was well sighted on some rising ground within a *wied*, just where a marauder bent on a terror raid might be expected to sneak in low. "Why didn't you fire, sergeant?" He replied: "It's not yet six o'clock, sir!" It was three minutes to the hour!

Orders are orders, time is time. At that period ammunition was so very short, every round must count, and there must be sufficient in hand for that dire day that seemed to be almost inevitable. Almost; who knew? There was always a spirit of hope in these church-going islanders and a vast store of faith imbued by that Christian religion St Paul brought to the land all those centuries ago. Today they were led by their Archbishop, Bishop Maurus Caruana, and by the well-respected Governor, Lieutenant General Sir William Dobbie, that God-fearing "Ironside of a man", Churchill had called him.

Faith and hope. Also there was humour. An issue of tinned beans to augment the meagre rations brought forth mirth that immediately echoed round the island. Beans do to the Maltese what they do to everyone else — especially on empty stomachs. They fill them with wind. Even before the issue was announced the Maltese knew: "They are going to issue beans . . . we must be short of shells again . . . so everyone has to do his bit . . . they are to give us all a tin of beans." And the laughter echoed.

There was nothing in the shops. Only essentials reached the island — when anything did. Even the submarines, in addition to their marauding, patrolling and reconnaissance roles, brought in what they could when they could, especially high octane fuel for the aircraft. H.M.S. *Porpoise*, during fourteen months' service in the Mediterranean, called at least four times at Malta with essential supplies and aviation spirit, fully utilizing the space that would normally have been occupied by her torpedoes. On her flag she jocularly displayed the letters P.C.S. for Porpoise Carrier Service and added a white bar each time she successfully completed the visit to the island, it being considered by the crew as meritorious an achievement as sinking an enemy vessel. She was one of the largest mine-laying submarines of the Royal Navy and played a full part in offensive patrolling, surviving at least a hundred depth charges. A record her crew would rather not have experienced and which was unique in British naval warfare was the attraction of eighty-seven depth charges in four days. The *Daily Mirror* journalist Bernard Gray, mentioned by Hugh Cudlipp in *Publish and Be Damned*, used his initiative and presumably much influence to get to the island by smuggling in aboard an aircraft. He was not welcomed but was told by the Governor that the space he had occupied could better have been filled by a sack of potatoes.

He told the few of us who sometimes congregated near Fort St Elmo in Valletta of life in England, and brought over to us the feeling of home and the suffering there, too. But there was no disguising his belief that life in Valletta was no life at all and that the incessant pounding and almost continuous alerts must eventually break even the most staunch of spirits. He taught us 'When Nightingales Sang in Berkeley Square', and indeed his coming was a tonic. But he did not stay long. His news sense made him believe that there was some intense action building up in the Middle East and he was anxious to get there. How? He dare not ask even the Governor for help. After many attempts to get away he somehow managed to smuggle out aboard a submarine. He told me he was going but, alas, his Middle East assignment was never completed and a promising career was ended abruptly—the submarine was lost.

Valletta was no place to choose for relaxation, yet in some strange way it offered change and alternative companionship. It was a daily, and nightly, target for bombers but the bombardment there was somehow different among the high fortress buildings to the slit trench life around the airfields. The dirt and dust and the smell of the countryside could be exchanged for the sophistication of the Union Club (the Auberge de Province in badly bombed Kingsway) and the welfare atmosphere of the Command Fair—specially thought up and set up with a weekly music-hall show and minor side shows as an attraction to combat the boredom that infected many of the troops. The boredom and frustration of the infantryman at not being able to hit back. There were also bars and hotels but less and less in the way of refreshment as time went on; and less and less of actual opening time as the raids increased in frequency.

I believe that most people, consciously or subconsciously, had made a reassessment of existence values. Life was sweeter than worldly goods, comradeship more natural than solitude. There was greater understanding of one's neighbour, his strengths and his weaknesses. And weakness was allowable. We each had our own, while aiding others gave us each some strength. We were all in it together and depended one upon another.

I cherish the memory of the proprietor of a hotel in Valletta. Both he and his wife were friendly and helpful, as far as they were able in the days of shortage and hard rationing. Both answered the call of the siren as though they knew it heralded doom and went to their deep-dug shelter immediately it sounded. Nothing brought them up again except the all-clear. A few of us visited on occasion and congregated in the bar. We, brave or foolish souls that we were, never used their shelter but would sit in the bar and talk until the raid was over. The landlord had no hesitation in leaving the bar open and the till free. We took what drink we needed, paid up and never bilked.

One night, arriving late during an air raid, I slept on the front door step in my tin hat while shell splinters sh-phlutted through the air to make their distinctive little tinkle-ding as they hit the road. No amount of knocking would get the landlord out of his shelter while a raid was on and I knew it. And there is no doubt that his wise, uncompromising precaution saved his life and that of his wife. One Saturday I arranged to be at the hotel in the early afternoon to meet Bill Taylor, a captain in the Manchesters and one of the organizers of the Command Fair. At midday I collected my bicycle and was about to move off from Mqabba when the alert sounded. I had to cross the Peter and Paul road junction of the Luqa-Safi strips and so I first waited for the normal telephone call advising of the possible area of the raid. It was Luqa and the plot: "90 plus".

I decided to wait until they had gone by but when nothing had happened after half an hour I began to wonder if I would be late for my appointment and moved off warily. Just before reaching St Peter and St Paul the bombers came in. It was Luqa they were aiming for and I dived for a ditch. It was like watching an express train scream through and when they had gone I remounted my cycle and hurried over the crossing to continue my way to Valletta.

There I found that the city also had been visited. As I walked down Merchant Street I could see a mass of rubble heaped right across the road and my rendezvous hotel had been cut right out from the buildings right and left of it. I thought of Bill Taylor and as I stood contemplating he suddenly appeared from the midst of the ruins, slightly dishevelled, carrying a suitcase in one hand and a bottle of Johnnie Walker whisky in the other. "Are you all right, Bill?" I shouted. "Aye!" he answered, waving the bottle. "I saved it!" And a Maltese policeman, picking his way across the rubble as he made his way down the road, quite casually and naturally said: "And still going strong!" Yes, instant *camaraderie*, understanding, humour.

RED FLAG

Oh, a-rollicking round the harbour,
A-rollicking round the town,
With never a landlord's daughter
And never a girl in brown.
A-dodging the ack-ack splinters,
A-looking for wine and song.
The red flag's up! The red flag's down!
Oh, now we won't be long.

The landlord's moving the shutter,
The landlord's smiling wide,
The landlord's over the doorstep
And beaming "Come inside."
The landlord's fetching the whisky,
But we've been sold a pup,
The landlord's turning the key again,
The red flag's going up.

Here too, in Valletta, the people clung to their known homesteads although much of life was spent in the shelters. Thousands had evacuated from Valletta and the Three Cities across the Grand Harbour and from other towns, too, when the savagery and horrifying effect of the continuous torrent of bombing was realized but, strangely, many thousands remained. The city was well planned after the 1565 Turkish attack and the promontory between the two harbours was levelled to provide a symmetrical criss-cross pattern of streets surrounded by the huge bastions, ramparts, cavaliers and curtains of the fortress, with on the landward side a mighty ditch. But in spite of the planning it is very much a city of steps. Byron remarked on this, as a visitor notices oddities and eccentricities, but none noticed it nor cursed it so much as the war-harassed residents themselves. Especially the halt and elderly. It seemed strangely idiotic to most of them that in order to go down into a deep safe underground sleeping place one first had to climb up twenty, thirty or forty steps. Many, of course, lived in flats, five or six flights up from the street door, so it was a long way to the shelter. Down, up and down again.

Nevertheless, such is habit and the homing instinct, that all would go to their own hole rather than seek refuge in another closer shelter when caught out in the open. Once I descended from a bus near the entrance to Kingsway (now Republic Street). At that instant a bomber swooped with a nerve-scratching screech and there was a tremendous crash and an immense ball of billowing yellow-grey smoke and dust as a bomb exploded a bare hundred yards away in the ditch under the high city walls. A young lady rushed towards Kingsgate (now City Gate) into the area just bombed. "Wait," I shouted, "go to the shelter until the bombers have passed!" She refused impatiently, and so incongruously in the midst of raining death: "My mother! I must see if she has got to her shelter!"

Valletta is a vast warren of underground chambers, so I said: "Go down here and make your way through!" "No!" she replied. "It is quicker through the town . . . I've got to find her!" So we walked and ran nearly a mile while the raid continued, picking our way past the demolished Opera House, the Castile and the Barrakka and down those interminable sloping, slippery steps in St Ursula Street. In the event her mother was safe. Such emergencies and common dangers drew people together in this land of siege. So it must have been at Troy and undoubtedly was in that great *camaraderie* under the fire bombs of London.

VALLETTA: CITY OF STEPS

Steps! steps! steps!
Forever climbing steps.
Up in the morning and down at night,
Hurry and scurry with all your might.
Steps! steps! steps!
Worn ones and new ones,
Torn ones and true ones.
Steps! steps! steps!

Steps! steps! steps!
Silvery slippery steps.
Into the shelter without any light,
Tripping and skipping down the last flight.
Steps! steps! steps!
Stone ones and wood ones,
Bad ones and good ones.
Steps! steps! steps!

Steps! steps! steps!
Solemn and stately old steps.
What do you see in the watch of the night?
"Lovers and bombers and flashes of light."
Steps! steps! steps!
New ones and used ones,
Bombed ones and bruised ones.
Valletta's immortal steps.

In what is now Freedom Square, close by Victory Street, I
had on another occasion seen a policeman calmly walking
with an armful of anti-personnel stick bombs, nonchalantly
picking up others as he went on his way. These were new to
the inhabitants of Valletta and I think the Italians must have
forgotten to arm them. How else could the industrious policeman have survived or I be here to tell of it today?

As in Britain the wailing siren heralded each air raid and
the long, steady note signalled its close. Over the Rediffusion
system came the rapidly spoken incisive command, thrice
urgently declared in Maltese and English: "*Twissija Ta Hbit
Mill Arja!* Air Raid Warning! Air Raid Warning! Air Raid
Warning!" On vantage points in Valletta red flags were
hoisted as a visual warning. In this city especially was it
imperative to shelter against bombing, but as the raids
became longer and more frequent it was almost impossible to
work if one obeyed every siren's call. Not all raids meant
bombing, some heralded fighters or reconnaissance planes.
Not all planes were directed at Valletta, though the island
was so small one really never knew where the next delivery
was to be made.

However, a new flag signal was devised. A red and white
flag meant fighters were heading for the city. Red meant

bombers. The flag stations were on the Governor's Palace (Government headquarters) and the Auberge de Castile (Army headquarters). Most people waited for the red before going to shelter, but few could see the flags and relied on word-of-mouth information.

Boy scouts had been of enormous use and shown keenness and bravery as messengers in the Dockyard, indeed nearly 1,000 were awarded the Scouts' Bronze Cross during the war, but in Valletta even smaller boys found a task to their liking and one that was a great help especially to older people. Using their own initiative the lads set up miniature signal stations with miniature poles and miniature flags. They took their cue from the main signal stations and hoisted their flags when danger showed. They put their own lives at risk and never cried 'wolf'.

BEPPU JOE

Now there's them as talks about it,
But I wouldn't want t' shout it,
An' I wouldn't want t' tell yer all the story;
But there's this I'll say outright:
When it does come to a fight
Well the bravest doesn't always get the glory,

It was out there in the Medi
Where the porpoises play steady.
We was sittin' in a place they calls Valletta.
An' they kind o' made me rile
When they called it 'George Cross Isle',
Though I changed me mind when once I knew 'em better.

We would sit an' shade our eyes
While a-watchin' o' the skies,
An' a-waitin' fer the Boche t' drop 'is packet
An' we'd chase the little brats
Who came creepin' round like rats,
All the kids who came a-watchin' o' the racket.

There was one I liked the best,
But I chased 'im with the rest,
'Cos yer can't 'ave lots o' kids around the Bofors.
When there's duty t' be done
An' we feeds the ruddy gun
It means work, 'ard work; there ain't no time fer loafers.

Well, 'is name was Beppu Joe,
If yer really wants t'know.
'E was just another little ragamuffin.
'E wore little more than trouse's
But 'e never 'ad no grouses,
Just a lot o' sarc', a real an' reg'lar tough 'un.

Yes, our language gets most fruity
When we 'as t' do our duty,
An' I well remembers 'ow I used t' curse 'im.
Shoutin': "Go, yer little swine!
"Look, they're divin' in a line!"
But I wish I 'ad 'im now; my God, I'd nurse 'im.

When the bombs was droppin' fast
You could bet 'e'd be the last
T' leave the street. 'E never used t' slide out,
An' 'e'd never 'elter-skelter
Like the others int' shelter,
But 'e'd man' is 'ome-made cannon in 'is 'ide-out'.

Came the day I slipped an' fell
With a wound like burnin' 'ell
Where a bit o' singin' shrapnel came an' caught me.
'Course me mates they 'adn't time,
But *'e* saw an' brought me lime
Through th' shrapnel 'ail—that should've, ought'a taught me.

It really wasn't long
'Fore I come back fit an' strong,
An' a-burstin' t' bring down a reg'lar whopper.
An' I got a damn good shot in
At a bomber that was spottin',
Then 'e pulled the stick an' let us 'ave it proper.

Well, 'e missed us, as they do,
But I sort o' kind o' knew
That everything just wasn't bright and bubbly.
When the wind 'ad cleared the air:
God! 'is ''ide-out' wasn't there!
'E was buried t' 'is armpits in the rubbly.

We 'ad well night dug 'im out
When we 'ears a bloomin' shout
An' a lot o' feet just runnin 'elter-skelter,
An' 'e whispers: "Get t' . . . cover!"
An' I thinks: 'ere comes anover;
But I couldn't leave 'im and get int' shelter.

I remember 'fore I fell
'E said: "Allura, pal!"
Then smiled an' looked away — no fear, nor frettin',
— There's no George Cross where 'e's gone,
But the likes of 'im live on
And of Beppu Joe there's never no forgettin'.

EIGHT

The Miracle of Mosta

At Lija in a narrow, winding limestone lane that eventually leads to Ta'Qali there is a little wayside chapel named Tal Mirakli — The Miracle. It is close to a convent of the Sacred Heart where during the siege the good sisters carried on their work in spite of the bombs that fell around. Tal Mirakli is but a tiny room of God's House where wayfarers before the war would rest peacefully a while in the depth of the countryside. Where, too, goatherds and other country folk would pause to pray and hope, perhaps, for help in attaining their own miracles — increased crops for almost barren fields, children for barren wives.

Almost next door is Villa Alfano where I was to live with my family for a time after the siege, with goats once again being herded along the lane for their early morning milk delivery. The villa, small as it was, was a joy to my children Avril and David and a relic of the time of the Knights, entirely self-contained with its own indoor well, small orange grove, with high, six-foot thick, defendable walls and a one-time stables and bakery. Behind a miniature indoor chapel there was even a priest's hole where a fugitive might hide — albeit in standing position — and escape detection. The villa was also reputed to harbour a ghost, but we saw nothing. However, my wife Edythe — perhaps because she was Welsh — did not like being left alone with the 'presence' and what appeared in the shadows of early evening to be a pair of horns half hidden in a dark recess of the high kitchen ceiling. Perhaps the occasional, and therefore always unexpected, eerie cry of a peacock calling "A-a-av-ril!" from beyond the high walls of the house next door helped to produce a creepy feeling in the quiet and cool solitude, reinforced by a mournful echo from the uncovered well. However, the sweet-scented stephanotis around the kitchen door, the capers growing from cracks in the high surrounding wall and the colourful oranges and lemons catching the sunlight, all helped to conjure imaginative and happy thoughts of former occupants and bygone ages.

In such 'fortressed' houses the Maltese landowners of even tiny holdings have lived over the centuries, ever ready to defend family and freehold and to exist on those few crops that can struggle through the thin, rocky soil. In 1945 I was to experience great difficulty in obtaining the barest necessities to only partly furnish and equip this house with such items as beds, knives and forks, even two years after the siege was raised. Such were the shortages that persisted for some years after the nation's resources had been sought out and utilized down to the last thimble.

Tal Mirakli with its simplicity and faith is in a way the key to the real miracle that happened at Mosta on 9 April 1942. First, to set the background, let us consider the churches of Malta, the extent of the damage to houses and other buildings, and the casualties to the civilian population. Of the 300 churches and chapels 86 were badly damaged during the siege. This does not include those whose exterior walls are still scarred and will bear to eternity the pockmarks caused by bombs exploding in their vicinity. I think there cannot be one that does not bear the marks of war. In addition, 23 convents and nunneries were destroyed or damaged, as were 10 hospitals even though they clearly displayed large red crosses, 31 schools and colleges, and 3 cemeteries.

Of the tens of thousands of dwelling houses that suffered direct hits, were damaged by near misses or blast, 28,000 were badly affected. Some 10,000 of them were either totally destroyed or were so badly damaged that they had to be demolished before rebuilding could be commenced.

The high percentage of religious buildings attacked and critically damaged emphasizes how closely the bombing was taken to the people in the widely dispersed villages — attacks clearly intended to strike fear into the lives of the humble in preparation for that day of assault, already planned, practised for and code-named 'Herkules' by the Axis, that all, particularly the Italians, fully expected to be launched.

Considering the intensity of the onslaught, the long years of death-dodging continuity, and the routine-affecting and long, continuous raids disorganizing meals, work and sleep, the civilian casualties were not high; even though on a number of occasions the whole of the occupants of a village shelter were killed. Others had miraculous escapes after being entombed—in one case at Paola for two days, with water leaking in and rising. Here 18 out of 21 were saved. In the whole of the siege men outnumbered women killed, but only by a small amount: 687 to 422. The number of children who died by enemy action was comparatively high at 384.

There were nearly three times as many wounded, 3,764, with again a high proportion of children. The figures were: men 1,778, women, 1,066, children 920. The grand total of only 5,257 killed and wounded in three years of intense bombardment day and night demonstrates how a stricken populace can adapt to even the most terrifying conditions, can learn to take precautions, can exist in what would normally be unacceptable habitations, and can adjust to most unusual hours—even catnapping like some animals of the wild. It also emphasizes again the Maltese ability to survive through the centuries and the strength of the limestone in their character and in the rock that protected them.

The village churches of Malta are constructed to accommodate the whole village congregation. They are huge and built with loving care by the people, while treasured within them are the large, heavy statues of their saints which are laboriously progressed around the village during the appropriate *festas*. The village priest knows all—all the people and all their foibles. The church and the people are one—one community under God.

The bells of the churches ring out for all services and none can sleep late beyond the call for morning prayers, as visitors to Malta well know. But the urgent clangour of the bells was not heard during the siege, their voices being reserved for the dire warning of invasion. They were silent except for those of the church clocks, which never struck beyond six strokes—the hour of seven being recorded with one stroke, and so on. The clocks, striking heavily, solidly and solemnly in the hot summer nights, while restless sleepers kept one ear cocked for the ever-wailing siren, emphasized the absence of the great bells calling and re-calling to prayer. Yes, the church bells were silent, except on one memorable occasion when joyously and spontaneously, and without permission, they rang out when Tunis fell and 291,000 Germans and Italians surren-

dered to the Allies. That is the way of the Maltese — circum-
stances justify actions.

Each Malta church is different and distinctive, except that
Luqa and Naxxar are very much alike with their twin towers.
We of the garrison very soon knew each village by its own distinctive church and could recognize them from a distance,
for each church stands high above all the surrounding
houses, like a mother hen with her brood assembled. Indeed,
the church of Mgarr with its very high dome looks so appropriately like an egg. Its priest Father Salomone, later
Monsignor, and popularly known as Dun Edgar, had over
long years collected eggs and hens as offerings from his parishioners and taken weekly to the market in Valletta until
enough cash was raised to build the church.

The people of Mosta, also, raised the money to build their
own church and provided, too, the volunteer labour. It was
but seventy-eight years old when the miracle happened and
there were still a few who could remember it in its early days,
but the original church had been built over 300 years before.
The dome of Mosta church, in spite of its humble origin, is
the third largest in the world. At 118 feet in diameter it is
exceeded only by St Paul's Cathedral in London at 127 feet
and the Pantheon at 143 feet, a fact of which this village is
immensely proud.

The miracle occurred on 9 April when other villages also
were tortured in their faith. At about the tea hour some 300
parishioners were assembled inside the church awaiting the
early evening service. Suddenly the air-raid siren sounded
and shortly after the throb of planes could be heard
approaching. They had often done so in the past, flying
overhead to their airfield or harbour targets. So to the
waiting congregation the huge, solid, tough old church still
seemed a comparatively safe place. They waited in silence,
some in prayer.

Now the planes were overhead and suddenly there came a
piercing, shrieking whistle and a crash like a thunderbolt.
The whole huge auditorium was filled with dust and noise.
The people knew the church had been struck. They could not
see through the dense haze but it seemed to be falling about
them. In fear and bewilderment they fought to prevent
panic. Then daylight began to filter through the dome and

they dimly understood that a bomb had bounced and rolled along the floor of the nave. With realization they fought fear again and struggled as fast as they could towards the main door. As they rushed outside, gasping and blinded by the dust, and stood gathering sight in the daylight, then, in their agony, they saw another bomb beside the entrance. Having almost escaped the one they knew terror afresh. But neither exploded, nor in this miracle were there any casualties among the congregation. Except for the hole in the dome and the dent in the nave the damage to the church was minimal. Then, fearful for their church and unmindful of the dreadful risk they ran, some of the men began to manhandle the bomb out of the nave.

I have never heard this incident referred to as a miracle but I can find no other word nor explanation for it. The people of Mosta, humble in their thankfulness, declared that they were saved by the intervention of their own patron, Our Lady, to whom the church is dedicated. With 300 witnesses I believe there must be many today who would accept that this was indeed a miracle.

So many in Malta had so often prayed: "Oh Mother Mary spread your wide mantle that the bombs may not harm us . . ."

NINE

Village Tales

That fool Antonio! A name long associated with foolish Italians, but not to be confused with the respected and endearing Maltese-intoned Tonino, nor with the austere English Anthony. Of the latter more anon, but listen a while to these stories gathered from the villages. These are twice-told true tales. They were written at the time of the events. They amused or otherwise entertained us then and today I can find no better arrangement of words than the ones I used when the war was still around us. I have made only slight alterations merely to clarify and have included some additional facts that were not permissible then because of censorship. If these tales seem trivial now, maybe trivialities helped us through, but there was nothing trivial about dodging death, nor in taking reasonable precautions. Behind each of the happenings lay fear or foreboding, hope, steadfastness or daring, veiled in humour or understanding comradeship. Perhaps they may invoke something of the atmosphere of the time.

Birzebbuga

That fool Antonio! I was not living in Birzebbuga but nearby in a tiny hut right at the end of the runway at Hal Far, where the Fleet Air Arm Swordfish biplanes flew in and out all night on their missions of harassing and sinking Rommel's supply ships. The intrepid but unfortunate pilot of one of these machines blew himself up one night when the Swordfish came in and landed on its own torpedo which never disengaged during an attack operation and was held dangling with the warhead downwards. The plane seemed extremely low when it wobbled in over my hut in the small hours and the unlucky pilot must have known he had no chance of survival either by ditching or landing. But all that, sadly horrifying as it was, is incidental.

The Antonio incident always reminds me of the little

village of Birzebbuga tucked away by the *wied* that runs into the centre of Marsaxlokk Bay. It must be very difficult at times for night-flying Antonio to find the island. Such a small spot right out in the blue. And when there is no moon and there *is* cloud, and a rigidly enforced black-out — not a speck of light . . .

There was a certain amount of cloud tonight and no moon, and apparently the policy was 'Douse' for no search-light appeared when the raiders came over the island. They came and went for half an hour. No bombs were dropped. Apparently they could not see, they were not sure, or it was an aggravating nuisance raid; and we wondered just how long this was going on.

Then suddenly a parachute flare. Floating high like a great earth-bound star and slowly, slowly descending. If they could not find the island by any other light they intended to supply their own. But this flare was floating down over the sea at least half a mile from the coast. Still it was only a matter of time. One here and one there, bracketing and extending. Why did we not open up the lights and get him now? He was low enough in all conscience' sake.

But the next flare fell a mile further out to sea and the next two miles . . . We lost interest. Antonio, what a fool!

Here is another near miss that from Britain's point of view might have ended disastrously. When Anthony Eden, as Churchill's Foreign Secretary, visited Malta for a brief stop on 13 October 1940 *en route* to the Middle East, his pilot too failed to sight the island — which says much, not only for the policy of 'Douse' and the effectiveness of the black-out, but also for the radio silence that was probably intended to safeguard the VIP. Fortunately the pilot turned about in time with very little fuel left in the tanks and discovered the tiny speck that both Mussolini and Hitler tried so long and so hard to eradicate.

FLARES BY MOONLIGHT

(While the raid was on, with all lights out in the Mess, one of us played—the Moonlight Sonata.)

Moonlight Sonata! With this damned full-blown orb
And various hanging lamps a-drifting fast
Towards me and towards!
Moonlight Sonata! . . . How I hate the moon.
Cold, pale, bloodless. And yet bloody lust
Shines in her lifeless eyes. Moonlight Sonata!

Beethoven, could you now sit and write
Sonatas here beneath these cloudless skies?
With Boche flares glaring and with that moon staring?
Bombs bursting, guns flashing, stones and earth spattering?

Moonlight Sonata! God! . . . and yet
It still has power to hold me. Let the Boche
Pound on and make his devil's din
Blast his own soul to hell.

Mqabba

This was the day the first Spitfires arrived. They came in during an alert. I do not remember any enemy planes over the island, but these new shapes certainly surprised us when they swooped in so swiftly and so low, almost like elated, mischievous darting schoolboys.

Things have to be kept secret about an island so close to the enemy. Especially when the enemy is so attentive and especially when you contemplate delivering goods. Even though you do not actually have to go to the doorstep, the goods being able to fly the last few miles and deliver themselves. We had heard rumours that they were coming—things do leak out—but we were not going to believe it until we actually saw them. We had very few of the older Hurricanes left now and although they had done a sterling job they were too slow. And they were so very, very few. The Boche had hundreds of bombers and fighters and he was pounding and pounding, hammering and hammering. We were just taking it. And the cry was: "Give us the tools . . . !"

The first to see them was a small boy. He had never seen one before, but he knew! We looked in amazement as they came in low at a rattling pace—we had never seen anything so fast. They flashed in, circled and landed. And the whole village took up the cry of the small boy. I can still hear him and them laughing, jumping, gesticulating wildly: "Spitfires! Look! They're here. Marija! They've come! Spitfires! Now we'll show 'em! Spitfires! Spitfires!"

And as the world now knows, they did show them. Even as soon as two hours later they were taking their toll. While those who knew the wavelength were listening in and were thrilled when they first heard the anxious tone of a surprised Boche pilot screaming: *"Achtung! Schpitfeuer!"*

Dingli

I tapped on a door in the village of Dingli when the food shortage was most acute and, heaven forgive me, I asked for bread. The door was the door of a very small cottage. I knew the inhabitants, they were my friends. I meant it only as a joke and expected to be recognized at once with a laugh. But it was dark outside, all Army overcoats look the same and I suppose I was in the shadows. Black-out regulations were stringently observed in those days, even at Dingli far from any likely target. When the door opened no light shone on me.

I heard: "A soldier asking for bread." A pause and then came a hand through the aperture and a thick slice was passed out. "Here, take this, Joe—the best we can do—*il-lejl it-tajjeb* [sleep well]."

I felt my duplicity keenly. For although they were soon laughing heartily at a joke against them, I knew that they had unhesitatingly given up a portion of their ration when bread was very scarce. They were giving it up to a fighting man because they imagined him young and hungry and . . . they knew what hunger was.

LULLABY: MALTA 1942

"How many Junkers are coming tonight?"
If I knew my dear I'd tell you right.
Now off with your clothes and brush out your hair,
Then down to the shelter. They can't hurt you there.

"How many things did they break at Aunt Jean's?"
Oh how should I know? She tidies and cleans
And the place is as bright when they've gone on their way
As ever it was on an old festa day.

"How many bombs was it knocked down the church?"
Oh dear, Mary child, where's the pin? Let me search.
I don't quite remember. I think it was six.
Now stop all your questions and finish your tricks.

"And when will my Daddy come home from the war?"
Now stop traipsing child, get up off the floor.
He'll come very soon now the Hun's running fast.
Now, shelter! Thank goodness you're ready at last.

Mosta

I have no reason to believe that this is a libel on a fair village.
It was told to me by one of the inhabitants who vouched for
its truth—and, if any one did, he should know. The raid was
finished but the all-clear had not yet sounded. Father was
leaving the shelter as would an advance guard or scout to see
if the house was still standing and if otherwise the route was
clear. But Father did not leave the shelter—he came rushing
back with the news: "There's a bomb at the top! Not far from
the entrance! Nobody can leave—everyone must stay here!"
Father, who had been listening meekly to all the old wives
talking for the past hour, Father had taken command.

Now to save his brood. Acting against their tearful
entreaties he walked up the steps, took one look at the 'bomb'
and rushed by: to the A.R.P.—to be told they had other jobs
on their hands; they would come later. To the police—yes,
they would come along later, too. Anyway, what could one
do about an unexploded bomb? There were UXBs all over
the island, the Bomb Disposal Squad was dealing with them
and this one would have to wait its turn, or go off. It would
be marked and ringed and would not hurt anyone as long as
they kept away from it.

Well, well, nothing to be done but tell them in the shelter
to stay put. So once again with a quick glance at the bomb
Father rushed by and down the steps. This time he reported

that he thought he had heard it ticking, but Mother, who was getting angry at being kept below, said it was possibly his own heart and perhaps she was more right than she knew. Or perhaps it was her womanly intuition based on a knowledge of her man that brought her near to the truth at that moment.

Twice more Father had to do the hundred yards in record time, once to get coffee and on the other occasion it was something to do with the baby. Each time he reported that there was a crowd at a respectable distance which agreed with his advice to "Keep them down".

After two more hours in the shelter Father essayed another peep out. The crowd had now become immense and some kind of 'big noise' had arrived. Whether he was a general, a high member of the Government or the Governor himself, I have never been able to discover. I only know what I am told and I am told that he, the 'big noise', sagaciously eyed the bomb, shook his head, promised the assistance of the Bomb Disposal Squad and went on his way.

After his departure interest in the bomb began to wane and, except for those still in the shelter, most people went home. Anyway the numbers were so reduced that a small boy was able to elude his parent's hand and take matters into his own. With a hop, skip and a jump he reached the 'bomb', tore it from the ground and beat it on the earth. Being made of cardboard it immediately crumpled. With an insolent whistle he flung it away and walked sedately home. It was the cardboard whistling attachment to a real bomb.

I know Father rather well but I have never been able to discover what Mother said—especially about his sense of hearing.

Zurrieq

Dead of night. Stillness. Clearness and starlight. No moon. Quietness over all. Suddenly the chimes of St Catherine's Church crash into the stillness—five deep notes for the hour and two higher for the half—eleven thirty.

Silence again, and the stars. Then in the distance, faintly, the first notes of the alert—*another* alert. Taken up gradually by sirens in all the villages. And sharply, suddenly by our own. A few voices, A few feet. Just a patter. No doubt most people are already in the shelters — sleeping there.

I go to the roof of the school. As an Army officer I find it the best place. I can overlook my command and also get a good view of the surrounding country. I pass the A.R.P. sergeant-major standing by, waiting. "Good night for them, sergeant-major." "It is, sir; if they can find it." The island, he means.

From the roof I can see all around. Open country to the left, with the villages of Qrendi and Mqabba in the distance. In front and behind and to the right of me the village of Zurrieq, with the church tower high above all, like a heavy mass, like a fortress.

Darkness, but for the stars. Not a man-made light any-where. The stars cast a faint glow which illumines the church just sufficiently for me to see it. It will be difficult for the Boche to find the aerodromes. Yes, the sergeant-major was right, it will be difficult for him to find the island.

Silence. Ten full minutes. No doubt the population is in the shelters. If they have any sense they must be. Look at the number of times this village has been hit. And the casualties. Just blind bombing. Dropping them and getting out. You *never* know where they will drop. And on a night like this!

Ah! Listen! Faint in the distance. No, it is not one of our night fighters — I would have heard it go up. Besides . . . Ah! Another and another! Must be four or five of them. No searchlights! Policy 'Douse'? Perhaps they won't find the island. Bru-mmph! . . . but they have.

Now the searchlights are up and the guns are barking and the noise begins to get deafening. Two planes in the beams and — suddenly I notice the port engine of one is afire. Just a little red glow — which slowly spreads. The plane keeps on its course, flying away into the distance — and the glow gets bigger.

Then the most marvellous moment of this night, a moment I shall never forget. So unexpected and yet I should not have been surprised. This village of quiet, this village which has been bombed so many times on nights like this . . . this village with its shelters, its silence . . .

As I stood on the roof I had felt so much alone; insignifi-cant; waiting for the sound of an express train and all hell to be let loose. The droning, circling planes, diving and climbing, screaming and scaring. Enough to scare the bravest hearts to shelter . . . but this village I suddenly realized was alive!

I saw the red glow burst into an orange ball which slowly, so slowly drifted to earth. And the village? From the rooftops came a long-drawn-out sigh: "Ah-h-h!" and then the roar of cheering. Roof watchers? Yes *the whole village!* I can see them still in the starlight as they move and wave and cheer. My God! What a tumult!

So much for the fallacy that this most bombed island goes to ground.

KIRKOP: THE SPIRIT OF MALTA

He can bomb us, he can rake us,
He can blast our homes and shake us,
But he won't destroy the spirit of the people.
If you feel inclined to doubt me,
Sideways glance and scoff, or scout me,
Go and take a look at Kirkop and its People.

There a street, a rubble heap.
There a woman with her sheep
And a goat or two, is walking near the steeple.
Though there's not much road to walk on
There are lots of things to talk on
Down at Kirkop, if you like to talk to people.

There the flowers still are growing,
Though the bombers come a-sowing.
"When the siren wails we have to rush and scatter
"And we get down in the shelter
"Pitter patter, helter skelter.
"We're in the target and his bombs can shatter.

"If you've ever seen our village,
"Seen our church, our streets, our tillage,
"In the days before the Boche made war on childer,
"You will know why we are holding
"Firm of heart to stones and moulding,
"Standing by to build it up when times get milder."

All of Malta's had its trials,
And they're written in the files,
But we'll take a darned sight more than he has given,
For our children's happy laughter
Still resounds, and what we're after
Is a better, safer world for them to live in.

He can bomb us, he can rake us,
He can blast our homes and shake us,
But he won't destroy the spirit of the People.
If you feel inclined to doubt me,
Sideways glance and scoff, or scout me,
Go and take a look at Kirkop and its People.

Balzan

This is the story of the soup. I was invited to look in at any time and when I did I was pressed to stay to supper. A little while ago I would have refused or I might have taken some sandwiches with me, but the ration *has* increased lately and I thankfully accepted the invitation.

Yes, the ration has increased and they have started giving us potatoes again. Also, they have rationed other vegetables. We all get our chance now to buy fresh vegetables twice each week and at a reasonable price.

But about the supper. It was soup and it contained cabbage finely chopped and I was told the story of it. Of how the daughter of the house had stood in a queue from 8.30 to 12.30 and had then been relieved by a friend. After lunch she had stood again until 2.15 when she had had her ration weighed out for her. The vegetable ration for four people for half a week was . . .

"What do you think? They're so pleased with me—one whole cabbage!" Mummy did not fret and fume and wonder how she was going to make it go round. She received it with thanksgiving: "Marija Madonna, how thankful we are for these little things. Oh, the Italians, how they betrayed us—they will surely suffer more than we." Beside, all Mummy could get last week was a few sprigs of cauliflower.

I remember how before the war the English housewife used to test and reject, scrutinize and exclaim over cauliflower after cauliflower and "they must not break up in the pot". Last week Mummy was able to get a few sprigs.

And that is the story of the cabbage in the soup. But do not get me wrong. The amount of vegetables per person may be small but everyone now gets a fair share weighed out and, after all, fresh vegetables are always preferable to those 'de-hibernated' ones we used to get at the Victory Kitchens.

Mdina

In striking contrast to the story of the Mosta 'mine' is this one of Mdina. I was not present, thank heaven, but it is now common knowledge and I am told that I know at least one of the participants. But their names may not be whispered for fear of the trouble they may reap. Of its truth there is no doubt.

Huge sea-mines have been dropped at the entrance to the harbours and, as we know, some fell on the city of Valletta and did tremendous damage. Some, too, dropped at Mdina, although it is so far inland. One of these failed to explode.

I would have thought that any normal person would leave well alone when it comes to unexploded bombs and mines, but not so two or three intrepid youths. They coveted the glittering green silk parachute. Besides, clothing was scarce and what cannot you do with parachute silk?

To cut a long story short they not only coveted it but they acquired it. With what amount of wriggling discomfiture and idiot foolhardiness they alone know, for they had to dodge watching authority as well as risk their lives. What *we* know is the puzzlement of the Bomb Disposal Squad who next day had to solve the problem, not only of why the bomb did not go off, but also how it lost its parachute in mid-air or why it was jettisoned without one. And if so what sort of mine it was.

After all a sea-mine in the middle of an island is one thing but a sea-mine without any visible means of support, that does not dent the earth when it lands, is an entirely different kettle of fish—if you understand what I mean, and will excuse the metaphor.

When this story was first published in *The Sunday Times of Malta* I was sent anonymously a long piece of green silken

cord from the well prized parachute and retain it still as one
of the mementoes of the siege. Another is a silk handkerchief
made from part of a white parachute that saved the life of a
young German pilot near Ta H'las Church. As he floated to
earth soldiers of the Malta Pioneer Group converged on him
from all directions. He flung his pistol from him while still in
the air and, much to his astonishment, was brought in
unharmed.

TEN

Faith and Endurance

As the siege progressed through 1942 into the third year the things we had always looked upon as the necessities of life began to disappear. Clothing wears out, crockery breaks, iron rusts away, but with a given number of people and a sufficient number of, say, knives and forks, surely it is possible to maintain the *status quo*.

It did not work out like that. The number of families did not increase—in fact, there was a fall of over 2,000 in the population in 1942, due to a higher death rate, a lower birth rate and a higher rate of infant mortality, the effects undoubtedly of the bombing and the debilitating siege conditions. But even though the population decreased there was no lessening of the demand for cutlery, beds, tables, mattresses and blankets. People continued to buy as we do today, without thinking that supply might end. A box of matches, a gramophone record, a pair of socks, or wool to make them with are purchased when required without thinking, in the natural course of our free standards of living.

In Malta, quite suddenly we noticed that there was nothing in the shops. No doubt it was a gradual process but it became impossible to buy even a safety pin—which, if you think of it with due consideration for a moment, is in itself a real minor tragedy. What would life be if there were no more safety pins or even a humble pin? It happened in Malta. There had been no desire to hoard, no incentive to keep up with the Joneses or the Schembris, but it was most disconcerting to need a pair of shoelaces, a yard of elastic or tape, a tube of toothpaste or a box of drawing-pins and find that they were absolutely unobtainable.

I bought the last handkerchief for sale in a shop nestling under the shadow of the high walls of the Citadel in Victoria, Gozo—there were none in Malta. I was lucky to be ordered with my command, D Company of the Hampshires, for a short period of duty in the sister island which is about one quarter the size of Malta. We were billeted in the village of

Xewkija and found the people hospitable and, at that time, hardly touched by the war. There had been little bombing and our few weeks' sojourn was probably intended as a rest from the continuous bombardment of the airfields at Luqa, Safi, Qrendi and Hal Far, all of which we had experienced. In one month alone, April 1942, the island was on the receiving end of 6,730 tons of bombs and the strafing was so intense that the seventy Spitfires that came in on the aircraft carriers *Eagle* and *Wasp* had all been damaged and made unserviceable within three days.

Our Southern Infantry Brigade of the Hampshires, Devons and Dorsets guarding the southern corner of the island had felt the impact of at least 2,000 of those 6,000 tons, a high proportion for a relatively small zone even though we were sitting around the airfield of Hal Far, the developing strip of Safi and on the edge of the dispersal area of Luqa. Every building in our charge that was not shattered was damaged or pock-marked, while the roads and fields were patchworked with craters and filled-in craters and spattered with burnt-out planes, parachute flares and pieces of metal from damaged aircraft.

But to return to the shortages which had become so acute in Malta. It was impossible to buy so many things including bedsteads and bedding, although these could be hired at a price. Crockery and drapery were unobtainable, so too were envelopes, writing paper, a reel of cotton, ink—there were no throw-away ball-point pens then—a gramophone record which could ease tedious hours, even a packet of needles. Life became more and more centred around grandma who had always been careful, thrifty and provident.

Many found a new interest in the classics when this was the only literature still on the shelves of bookshops. But these old best-sellers, too, soon disappeared. Paraffin, the staple heating and cooking fuel, was a precious fluid that had to be queued for at rare intervals. This was a long, time-wasting procedure new to the Maltese but another one of those things which they soon learned to patiently endure. And patience was necessary, for queues of 300 and 400 and more would form—waiting for a barrel on a rickety wooden cart with a little slow-running tap, as though there was no urgency and all of today and tomorrow. If a raid developed when the paraffin man with his donkey cart was around then all went to the shelter, including the paraffin man. The donkey stood alone watching over the hundreds of oil cans left in a long winding snake to hold the places. There was mutual trust when death lurked and leered.

The army used 'flash cookers', oil-soaked rags set alight and with a slow, steady drip of water falling on to them drop by drop, hence the 'flash' or splutter. I never knew before that water could be used to assist combustion and have since wondered about the vast quantities hosed on to burning buildings. Some made the flash cookers work, some did not. Clothing and food were rationed in ever-diminishing quantities. Water, too, was short, for the Boche bombed the reservoirs. Malta hardly ever has enough water, even in the rainiest of winters.

Oddly, on this besieged island cut off from the world, even money became scarce, particularly small change. The Government printed notes of small denomination down to one shilling (five pence today, five cents in Malta). Coppers could sometimes be purchased at £1 for 19s. 6d. worth and local bars issued their own written IOUs for tiny amounts. Service messes had monetary paper chits down to one penny printed in book form for internal use. At this time it cost only one penny to send a letter and there were still farthing stamps for postcards.

The bulk of the populace did not have radio sets and there was no broadcasting station in Malta, but this did not deter a 'Lady Haw Haw' operating from Italy in an endeavour to seduce loyalty on the island. Her efforts met with ridicule and rancour. As also did the outpourings of lies, half-truths and sarcasm initiated from Rome Radio by one doleful Ansaldo. "Woe! woe! Ansaldo" the Maltese called him and never believed a single word he uttered. Such is the self-defeating effect of propaganda broadcasting when once a lie is caught out. The local Rediffusion system connected by landline to many homes disseminated news, air-raid warnings, announcements and some entertainment. It also fed loudspeakers set up in the central public squares of the towns and villages. These are the normal promenading and gossiping areas which in ordinary times are filled every evening with young strollers and older watchers, chaperones and talkers.

In Valletta the assembly area for young and old was Kingsway, now Republic Street, which today has returned to its old routine and closes to traffic each evening to be thronged and given over to gay laughter and banter.

Fuel for transport was in short supply. Bus routes were curtailed and buses reduced in numbers and many people walked to work, taking cover in the nearest ditch as bombers and fighters struck. Buses, too, would stop for local bombing while the travellers scattered. The roads to Senglea were blocked with debris early in 1942 and the area was supplied by sea across the hazardous Grand Harbour.

The meagre rations were gradually reduced to the hunger line. Foodstuffs that were rationed but not always available included sugar, rice, flour, edible oil, tea, milk or milk powder, bread, cheese, macaroni, pulses, corned beef, toilet and washing soaps, coffee, fats, tinned fish, tomato paste, matches, paraffin. Chocolate, jam and other such 'luxuries' had long been unobtainable. The rationing of bread and macaroni was the most disliked and the most necessary. The 'target date' of surrender was based on the store of grain for making bread. At 10½ ounces per day the bread ration was but a tiny fraction of the amount normally eaten. Vegetables were very scarce and expensive, though potatoes, when available, were subsidized.

One hot meal daily could be obtained from the communal Victory Kitchens at a charge of sixpence (2½ pence or 2½ cents today) and the surrender of part of the family ration. Goat was sometimes included in these meals but there had been no frozen meat for nearly a year and there were no cattle on the island.

CHILD OF THE BLITZ

One day last week the bombers came
And made an awful din;
But though they knocked the houses down
And stones came tumbling in,
They didn't wake Marija, 'cos
I held her to me tight.
She didn't know our shelter shook
And blast blew out the light.

She didn't know my puppy Nell
Was very, very scared,
And cuddled up so close to me
And whined, and stared and stared;
And couldn't understand at all
When dust came swirling in,
But sneezed and sneezed, and shivered when
They made that awful din.

Poor Marta she was crying 'cos
She'd left her toys behind;
And Johnny just sat looking and
He didn't seem to mind;
But when the bits fell from the roof
He gave an awful shriek,
And when the soldier held his hand
He didn't even speak.

Marija was as good as gold
She didn't hear the noise.
I tucked her in my little cot
With all my other toys
When all the bombers went away;
Then with my puppy Nell
We climbed out of our shelter at
The bottom of a well.

The few horses were being saved as the last beasts of burden
when petrol ended and for the last Victory Kitchen meal
before capitulation — but there were not many of them and
they were lean, hungry-looking specimens. When the crop
was sufficient, potatoes were used in bread-making and, in
due season, a few oranges would be issued for the children.
Sandals made with boxwood or rope soles and canvas uppers
proved usable, while dried leaves of lemon, fig and wild
strawberry were said to be a rather fragrant substitute for
tobacco. Some young ladies experimented with rice ground
very, very fine in place of the unobtainable face powder.

The brewing of beer ceased and the thirsty watched the
high Cisk brewery chimney at Hamrun daily for any signs of
smoke that might indicate a return to manufacture. The

adventurous searched for snails, but to the uninitiated, who probably collected the wrong species anyway, they proved tasteless and rubbery. Hunger was a real thing and a threat to the will to survive. Women went short so that their men could have sustenance enough to walk and work and that their children could survive. Then came epidemics of polio-myelitis, typhoid fever and scabies, while other diseases, such as scurvy, tuberculosis, enteritis and dysentery, were wide-spread, being the result of poor living conditions, shortage of food and irregularities of sleep.

Not only the civilians but the garrison, too, was stricken. Not desperately, but there was an isolation ward full of officer polio victims with badly affected limbs at Mtarfa Military Hospital. I was put among them. I had a fever and, apparently, the correct symptoms for they kept me there for six weeks. During which time I was reprimanded by the medical officer for answering the telephone—and they disinfected it, so they obviously considered me a possible case. However, there was nothing seriously wrong and after the unexpected but most grateful diet of a morsel of chicken for lunch for forty-two consecutive days and no visitors I was released to my unit.

Some of the polio cases had badly affected limbs and muscles and yet they all maintained a high morale with really boisterous spirits. Often when the sister's back was turned they would parade up and down the ward doing drill move-ments with broom handles for rifles even though their stiff arms and legs were strapped in awkward positions. Some of them were air crew and it was the depth of bad luck that these lads, most in their twenties, after successfully surviving the rigours of the siege and overcoming the enemy in air battle, should now be paralysed by polio.

In spite of the epidemics there was no panic among the population. The doctors seemed to take a firm hold from the beginning and the people did not know the full extent of the troubles, realizing that with weakness some disease must follow. I remember a call to my unit from an Mtarfa doctor for fleas. They were trying to trace the source of an infection. When I signalled company commanders to produce what they could from among their men they were most indignant and, I think, only one obviously dead flea in a match box ever reached Mtarfa.

Typical of the tightness of the siege, the difficulties of getting through to Malta and the determination of the Axis to destroy anything that did get in, was the Vian convoy in March 1942. Four merchant vessels escorted by a force of four light cruisers and nine destroyers under Rear Admiral P. L. Vian left Alexandria on 20 March. The cruisers were Vian's flagship *Cleopatra*, *Carlisle* and *Euryalus*, with the *Penelope* from Malta. The destroyers were the famous 14th Flotilla led by H.M.S. *Jervis*, *Kelvin*, *Kipling*, *Kingston* and *Legion*; also *Sikh*, *Havock* and *Hero*, with the *Lively* from Malta. The merchant vessels, which were to have an exceedingly rough, ill-fated passage, were *Breconshire*, *Talabot*, *Pampas* and *Clan Campbell*.

To assist the passage, aircraft from Malta and the Middle East bombed and harassed nine enemy airfields in Greece, East and West Libya, Crete and Sicily. In addition, the Army set up feint attacks in North Africa and the Royal Navy made a one-day air and sea attack on the island of Rhodes. All of these diversions were intended to pin down or otherwise extend forces that might be used against the convoy. Nevertheless, after the first uneventful day the ships were continuously attacked by hundreds of aircraft including torpedo carriers, high level bombing Junkers, and Stuka dive-bombers. On the surface two separate forces of Italian warships, including the battleship *Littorio*, three heavy eight-inch gun cruisers and six light cruisers with a shield of destroyers, converged to destroy the 40,000 tons of cargo. Their armament severely outgunned and outranged Vian's force.

In spite of the disadvantages, including redirecting and safeguarding the slow-moving convoy, Vian outmanoeuvred the superior forces firing against him and cheekily and daringly drove in to attack. His destroyers got close enough to put at least one and maybe two torpedoes into the battleship which, with its nine fifteen-inch guns, could and should have annihilated his command even from a range of ten miles. *Littorio* was also hit by cruiser gunfire, while an Italian cruiser was badly damaged and was later sunk by the Malta submarine *Urge*.

Meanwhile the convoy had changed course but was still

being subjected to devastating aerial attacks which at last destroyed one merchantman, the *Clan Campbell*, when only ten miles from Malta. A second, the *Breconshire*, was hit when almost 'home'. Malta was indeed home to *Breconshire*, a well-armed, fast naval supply ship that had on at least twenty occasions sailed in from Alexandria with much-needed materials, food and fuel. Her name and the courageous and repeated endeavours of her skipper, Captain C. A. G. Hutchinson, and crew, were among the legends that were growing in this tightening siege. Now *Breconshire* had sailed her last voyage but she would not go without making her own last valorous gesture. With destroyers, minesweepers and the two Malta tugs, *Robust* and *Ancient*, in attendance she was taken in tow and slowly eased towards Marsaxlokk Harbour on the southern coast. It took sixteen hours dodging mines and under repeated aerial attacks before she was secured in shallow water and left to settle on 25 March.

Breconshire has a revered place in the Malta story. She had brought so much to the island, had made the run a score of times alone, and now was caught when in protected convoy. In Marsaxlokk she was still subjected to heavy bombing and as she died she did not fail, for much of her cargo and fuel oil were saved as she rested with decks awash.

In retrospect, it was inevitable that *Breconshire* must go at last. None could have diced with death so many times without one, the fateful throw, going against them. So had it been with countless aircraft and their pilots who knew the tremendous odds. So would it still be with planes and their crews and with ships and the men of the sea.

With two of the four merchantmen delivered to Grand Harbour, Vian's force left Malta, but that was not the end of the affair for the Luftwaffe. From 24 March heavy air attacks began on the newly arrived vessels and soon both *Talabot* and *Pampas* were sunk, also in shallow water which allowed much of their cargoes to be salvaged. Men of the Cheshire Regiment, whose machine-guns helped to guard Grand Harbour, were among those who played a wet, dirty, gallant part with the dockies in the recovery, working day and night until the job was done.

This was one of the Luftwaffe's fiercest attempts to sink merchant ships in harbour and it continued right through the

Soldiers loading and making up belts of cartridges for Spitfire guns

Army and R.A.F. get together and control and dispatch to the needed spot on the aerodrome

Soldiers filling in bomb craters on an aerodrome

Soldiers building an aircraft pen, using stones from bombed buildings

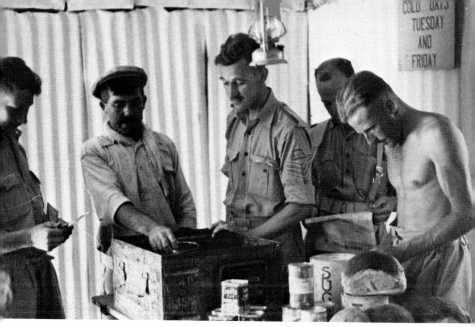

In the cookhouse the rations are checked. The 'cold days' were to save fuel

The girls of Malta's Fighter Control, after long hours in the underground Operations Room, would practise dance routines

Convoys on their way to Malta. *Above* The sky is filled with bursting anti-aircraft shells. *Below* A near miss – but this merchant ship reached Malta safely

A merchantman of the August 1942 convoy in Grand Harbour

Unloading *Rochester Castle* of the August 1942 convoy

SS *Talabot*, 7,000-ton merchant vessel, almost fully laden and with cargo ablaze in Grand Harbour on 25 March 1942

Old Bakery Street, Valletta, 7 April 1942. The city lay between Grand Harbour and Marsamxett – frequent targets for the bombers

A street in Senglea in January 1941 after the Luftwaffe's unsuccessful attempt to sink the aircraft carrier H.M.S. *Illustrious* in Grand Harbour. Although the ship survived, a large part of the Three Cities was destroyed

Clearing the rubble of bomb-wrecked buildings from a street in Valletta

Although blitzed and blasted, there are still signs of life in this corner of Senglea

The Opera House, Kingsway, Valletta,
7 April 1942

Valletta 1942

A flower-seller in Kingsway, Valletta

Caught by bombers on the road to
Sliema

Easter period. For the Force K cruiser *Penelope* also had been hit and was in Grand Harbour like a sitting duck, standing high in dry dock for urgent repairs. The repeated savage attacks, including dive-bombing Stukas through the hottest barrage, now concentrated on *Penelope*. They almost exhausted the crew and the guns and made the repair task of the dockies well nigh impossible.

Army welders came in to help and the tremendous effort to get the ship back to sea was truly a united endeavour. In the eleven days from 28 March to 7 April the gunners of *Penelope* alone fired over 5,000 four-inch shells and 75,000 rounds of smaller calibre. When they were running out of shells they loud-hailed for more and other vessels rushed them ammunition. The ship's company composed and sang their own special 'Shooting Song' to pep the gunners — who did not need it but appreciated the concern. People around the harbour area were amazed when they heard the sailors' voices raised in lusty unison while bombs burst, bombers roared, the ack-ack crackled and wounded men fell one by one. The harbour barrage was enormous but the attack was so fierce that it was amazing that *Penelope* did not suffer a direct hit.

Nevertheless, the many near misses which exploded all around the dry-dock area covered her decks with debris including chunks of rock up to half a ton in size until her quarter deck was referred to as the 'rock garden'. Her sides were pierced with hundreds, even thousands, of holes which earned her the name *Pepperpot Penelope*. When she left harbour to sail through to Gibraltar, which she reached safely, the holes had been temporarily plugged with what appeared to be a thousand broomsticks, so that she might more aptly have been called *Porcupine Penelope*. However, the name *Pepperpot* stuck — an epic episode and a famous ship.

Her gunnery officer was killed during the action and many of her crew in addition to the skipper, Captain A. D. Nicholl, were wounded. He was cheered to the echo when he limped back from the dressing station, refusing to go to hospital, just in time to sail the wounded *Penelope* away. That she should escape, filthy, lame and leaking but still living, was accepted as a victory by the hard-struggling

Maltese. The four merchantmen had been sunk, though something from their cargoes had been saved, but *Penelope*, brave *Penelope*, had fought well and got away. Malta was a base to fight from and not sit about in—as the Maltese knew quite well.

It was during this period that the 'children of the regiment' suffered their own particular ordeal. Not alone, but with their British mothers and with British naval and British civilian families—and simultaneously with the wounded, the sick, the doctors and the nursing sisters of a nearby military hospital that, under the rules of war as set out in the Geneva Convention, was exempt from aggression.

Early one morning shortly after the sinking of the ships in harbour and the survival and escape of *Penelope*—during which the people of Valletta also suffered so terribly—a pall of smoke and dust from bombs and crashing masonry was seen rising over the coast some two miles to the north-west of the city. The frightening, screeching sounds of dive-bombing could be heard, intermingled with the chattering of machine-guns and the pom-pom-pom-pom-pom of Bofors. There was always someone somewhere under attack and tension, but this was a barren, rocky area just beyond the inhabited suburbs of Sliema, St Julians and Spinola.

A glance at the map and a quick compass bearing pin-pointed the open area of Pembroke rifle ranges. Close by, we knew, were three British barracks, St George's, St Andrew's and St Patrick's—the latter converted into a temporary military hospital to augment the permanent Army one at Mtarfa, on the Mdina ridge in the centre of the island, and the naval hospital at Bighi right in Grand Harbour. The smoke was probably drifting from the barracks area but the soldiers of British regiments who in peacetime would have been living there were now, of course, occupying small posts and defensive positions in many parts of the island. Nevertheless—and this was the agony—their wives and children were in married quarters in the area. Also concentrated there were some naval families and some families of British civilians employed by the Services.

It was barely 7.30 a.m., with many of the children still in bed, when the first bombers struck, but most of the mothers had time to gather their youngsters and to reach their shelter or slit trench — some had only that slight protection — before the intensive bombing started. Most of them were in their night attire. Observers from a distance could see only the enlarging pall of smoke, feel the shock of the bursting bombs and praise the gunners for their protective efforts. Few realized the plight of unsupported women and children, but there were many husbands who watched with horror knowing that their families were in dire peril and that they could do nothing to succour them. It would, indeed, be several days before leave would be granted. It is at such times that the female of the species finds strength, ability and nerve to endure, to struggle and to protect her offspring unto death or survival.

This was a systematic attack with wave after wave of aircraft and with but short lulls between the bombing runs. The hospital was clearly marked with huge red crosses, even on the roof. These were hit in the first run — either by chance or intention — so Army nursing sisters, orderlies and even a German pilot patient, helped mark out fresh indications with red bed screens and blankets — but still the raids continued. The hospital suffered terribly under the fury of the attacks and the married quarters were demolished.

The women and children, clad for the most part in pyjamas, nightdresses and overcoats, suffered their torment and emerged from their shelters in thankfulness when the attacks finally ended. They could salvage little from the ruins of their homes, but in oddments of dress, even husbands' trousers, they set about making a communal home in their underground shelter. The 'lasses who follow the drum' of their husbands' regiments to all parts of the world are a tough breed who learn self-reliance and mutual support during their Service wanderings. On this occasion they showed a tremendous spirit of comradeship and fortitude, sleeping below in makeshift beds at night and feeding together in the open by day. Unlike the Maltese they had no relatives to move to and had all along been, more or less, an isolated community.

The Army helped them to adjust by arranging for sufficient tables, chairs and blankets and by providing food. One of their greatest difficulties was to acquire clothing. Ironically many had but recently given garments to the depots set up to help stricken Maltese families and were now so sorely needful themselves. It was hard enough to buy clothing now but it was not absolutely impossible. It was, however, difficult to get to Valletta and Sliema to make the rounds of the poorly stocked shops under the current bombing conditions and shortage of buses. It was foolhardy to take children on such hazardous expeditions but wives did not like to leave their youngsters in the care of others, partly because of their own protective instinct and partly because they did not want to overburden those who were already sufficiently worried by their own conditions. Many problems were solved when, after about the third day, husbands were granted passes for twenty-four or forty-eight hours. Then husband or wife cared for the family while the other shopped hopefully for the necessities.

So the families by St George's survived their own hour of concentrated attack and the 'children of the regiment' took it in their stride as youngsters all over Malta learned to do so competently. Today they are in their forties. How many remember this incident which at the time brought anguish to so many who were deeply concerned about their safety and welfare?

Such dramatic heart-rending events were among the trials and tribulations of the siege days that brought hope and then frustration and almost despair to the civilian population. On these occasions the world knew that ships had arrived and believed the food situation had been eased. It was not advisable to declare that the three arrivals had been sunk and thus gratuitously inform the enemy. Their high-flying reconnaissance planes might not be sure of this fact as the decks were still above water. Whenever a ship did arrive and the cargo was discharged intact the population naturally expected some addition to the food ration but seldom received any. A ship's cargo could bolster supplies to ensure endurance and that was the necessity: to continue to hold out and to hold on — to hold on to faith, hope, existence.

This was Malta in the siege years when Service personnel and civilians, men, women and children, strove together in order that the island and the freedom it personified should survive. The Maltese people in the direst days never wavered in their faith in God nor in their certain belief that right under the British would succeed. It was a hard, desperate endurance leavened by a fine sense of humour, clutching for and clinging to hope, and encouraged by achievement and a dedicated sense of purpose.

With their homes in ruins, the Boche still battering, even their churches stricken, hungry and sleeping fitfully when opportunity presented itself, careful of the few chattels that remained and mindful always of their children's safety, the people moved forward in 1942 still with a doggedness of purpose that was as strong and tough as the limestone rock itself.

How near they were to the target date when bread would run out and surrender would be inevitable they did not know. They only knew they must endure today and hope. So they tidied their streets after every smashing raid and hardened their ears to every crashing bomb. This was their life today. Tomorrow must show they had survived as had their ancestors who, too, had endured.

So they sat together in their darkened rooms and recounted ancient tales like that of the bride of Mosta, carried off on her wedding day and taken overseas by Muslim invaders, of the White Lady of Verdala, still appearing and scaring sentries at the Governor's summer palace, of the devil who turned into a black rock, and other stories of folklore and past heroes. New stories, too, of the heroes of the hour, of airmen like those in the Gold Coast Squadron, first to claim 100 enemy aircraft destroyed over Malta. Of twenty-year-old Canadian Flying Officer George 'Skewball' Beurling who, with single-minded purpose in fourteen days flying a Spitfire, destroyed twenty-seven enemy planes, probably destroyed three and damaged eight others. On 13 October 1942 he brought down the 1,000th plane destroyed over Malta and the following day shot down a bomber and four fighters and then successfully baled out of his own damaged, crashing machine.

They spoke, too, of submariners like the neat-bearded and well-liked Lieutenant Commander David 'Wankers' Wanklyn who won the Victoria Cross for his gallant exploits in *Upholder*. The marvellous record of this famous vessel and her dedicated courageous crew was reflected in the twenty-two success chevrons emblazoned on the Jolly Roger she flew when entering port after each mission. From her last she did not return and all Malta mourned.

All on the island talked, too, of the extremely hard working and relatively small squads of bomb disposal boys of the Royal Engineers and the Royal Army Ordnance Corps, two of whom won the George Cross. I attended the wedding of one, Lieutenant William Eastman, RAOC, when he married a Maltese maid. Bill and Yvonne still live in Malta. Lieutenant Eastman and his comrade in heroic endeavour, Captain Robert Jephson-Jones, RAOC, both eventually attained the rank of brigadier. Together, during the last six months of 1940, they safely defused at least 250 dangerous bombs — a tremendous achievement. One of their toughest was the horror that crashed with only inches to spare through the mouth of a well in Senglea. In cramped conditions, slime and tension they managed to rope it and had it hauled to the surface. They were each awarded the George Cross on Christmas Eve 1940 and received their awards from the hands of the King six years later.

Tales, too, of the heroism of policemen and gunners, of fears and frivolities and of those far-off pre-war days of *festas* and tranquillity. Of the seriousness of hooded penance and the dragging of heavy chains in Good Friday processions, of jollity in carnival time, of the annual national picnic in Boschetto Gardens, the Mnarja races at Rabat, and the rowing races in Grand Harbour.

It was good to think back sometimes — thinking forward was problematical. But there was not a lot of time to think. There was plenty to do and to work through today. This was a time of faith and endurance.

On 15 April 1942 His Majesty King George VI sent a signal to General Sir William Dobbie through the Secretary of State for the Colonies. It said simply, but with deep understanding and feeling: "To honour her brave people I award the George Cross to the Island Fortress of Malta to bear witness to a heroism and devotion that will long be famous in history. George R.I."

An honour unique to a community.

ELEVEN

Talabot Terror

It is worth moving back in time to take a more detailed look at the epilogue to what is now always described as the Vian Convoy. At this time Malta was desperately short of almost everything and was close to the starvation line that would herald capitulation. There was hardly any food left in store, aviation fuel was reduced to what was described as "the last few cans", while ammunition was so low that it was rationed to short bursts at definite times daily. That is why such a great effort was organized to get the convoy through and why so many diversionary assaults were co-ordinated in Africa, Rhodes and Sicily.

There always was a sufficiency of shells held in reserve to allow the garrison the greatest possible chance of repelling invasion but it was not the shells that would determine capitulation — it was the bread. No humane nation could allow the food stores for such a large population to reduce to the last crust. Too many would die in the weeks it would take the victors to bring succour and they would not hurry. With Malta reduced, their first consideration would be to give more support to Rommel. Moreover, the Italians were not feeding well and there would surely be repercussions if food was rushed to the now hated Maltese. The dictates of humanitarianism meant that surrender would be inevitable not when the bread was finished but when it had run so low that there was no chance of replenishment.

So the Vian convoy that so nearly succeeded — the Admiral had indeed delivered — was vital and the preservation of the cargoes aboard the ships that made harbour should have been absolute top priority. To some who watched the course of events at the time it seemed that there was a certain amount of lethargy and lack of urgency in getting the cargoes out. It was as though the 16,418 tons tightly packed in two merchantmen in Grand Harbour were considered to be in the larder and entirely safe.

The Luftwaffe had other thoughts, fostered by the realization that every ounce destroyed was a mouthful less to eat, a whimper nearer demoralization, and a second, a minute or an hour nearer their own success. It is true that the unloading went slowly but there was much justification for the delay. A ship's hold is a comparatively tiny place in which to work and only a certain number of crates and cases can be handled at one time. Moreover, instead of getting everything out and then sorting it, there was much shifting and selecting below decks to get out first what was considered to be most urgent. Under the heavy bombing the question, if it was asked at all, must have been: Do we ensure that the most vital is salvaged, or gather in bulk while we can and chance losing what we most direly need? It seems that the most urgently needed items were sought while time was fast running out. Another factor that slowed the unloading was that the crews of *Pampas* and *Talabot* were exhausted after their gruelling fighting struggle to win through from Alexandria to Malta. Their knowledge was necessary but they just could not push themselves any harder.

Then came the bombers. On the day of arrival, Monday 23 March 1942, there were heavy raids lasting 6 hours 39 minutes and as the derricks of *Pampas* were already damaged that cargo had to be unloaded by hand. Maltese stevedores took on the job. Next day, through the hell of seven air raids, 209 tons were unloaded from *Pampas* and 330 from *Talabot*.

Throughout the raids, of course, the now well-known harbour barrage was producing its own spectacular and adding to the devilish din. Bombs were falling everywhere and anywhere as the Spitfires and Hurricanes courageously and daringly struck at the attackers, spoiled their aims, diverted and chased. Shrapnel and shell fragments, cannon and small arms fire all combined to increase the hail of metal falling from the skies.

The large formation of enemy planes—thirty or more bombers at a time, escorted by screens of fighters—came in wave after wave. The Junkers 88 heavy bombers, Stuka dive-bombers and torpedo-carrying aircraft were coddled by clouds of Messerschmitt fighters above and around. The fast Spitfires took on the fighters, while the manoeuvrable Hurricanes attacked, diverted and otherwise harassed the bombers. The Malta planes were always outnumbered but never outclassed.

They fought heroically and the Luftwaffe paid dearly.

While the bombs breached bastions, battered buildings and missed the vital targets, there was an epic battle going on in the skies. It was the courage and determination of the airmen and the intensity of the gunners' barrage that forced Kesselring in Sicily to send in more and more planes to achieve his object—the sinking of two ships. Even so, it took the Luftwaffe three days to get a direct hit on either of the highly prized targets. Light and heavy anti-aircraft batteries and the guns of ships in harbour all combined to put up the most violent barrage the island had yet seen, while the Luftwaffe in wave after wave and raid after raid made one of the most vicious attempts to destroy the cargoes and in so doing neutralize Malta.

On the third day *Pampas* unloaded 310 tons, *Talabot* 497, and there were eight air raids. On Thursday 26th *Pampas* was at last hit, caught fire and started to sink, but another 280 tons had been discharged. *Talabot* had off-loaded another 145 tons when at 2.30 p.m. she, too, was hit and set on fire. This was serious for it was known that the vessel was carrying bombs and ammunition among her cargo. The only man on board at the time, and he had a remarkable escape, was Lieutenant Commander R. J. Knott, R.N.R., of whom more later. He was joined by Captain Stokes-Roberts of the Royal Army Ordnance Corps and together they fought the fire with a mobile foam extinguisher but failed to check it.

The tug *Ancient*, two fire floats manned by ratings from *Penelope*, and the local fire brigade with hoses run over barges to the blazing ship, attempted to subdue the fire, while the bombers now increased their concentration on *Pampas* and *Talabot*. *Ancient* and the fire floats were put out of action, some of the crews being blown into the sea. It was now early afternoon and ammunition in the hold of *Talabot* was beginning to explode. The ship's sides were red hot and there was growing fear not only for *Talabot* and the fire fighters but for the population of Valletta itself.

The black smoke rising several hundred feet above the harbour and the flames leaping from the vessel were an awesome sight, but the fact that there was ammunition aboard was quickly exaggerated, as rumours spread among the civil population, into "several thousands of tons". This was not true, but there was more than enough to make the authorities extremely concerned. Orders were quickly passed that the populace should remain in the deep shelters until the 'all-clear' sounded — and that would not depend on the presence of enemy aircraft but on the state of the ships.

As hour followed hour and the crowded shelters grew hotter and stuffier, only rumour and fear could gain credence. The sound of ammunition exploding could be heard even below ground and many recalled and passed the word of tremendous disasters that had and could happen to ammunition ships. They feared that the shelters that had stood them in such good stead against bombing might with one vast explosion disintegrate about them. They feared entombment. It is at such times that faith sustains the Maltese and led by their priests they prayed, recited the rosary and hoped. For six long hours they waited, just waited, knowing that they could do nothing to save themselves.

Meanwhile, in Grand Harbour under the pall of smoke that the Italians later said could be seen in Sicily sixty miles to the north, and under the continuing barrage and bombing, there were men calmly tackling the situation and risking their lives to solve the problem. His Excellency the Governor and Commander in Chief, General Sir William Dobbie, with the Vice Admiral Malta, Vice Admiral Sir Ralph Leatham, the Admiral Superintendent of the Dockyard, Rear Admiral Kenneth MacKenzies, and other senior officers decided that the ship must be sunk. This would not be easy to accomplish as her plates were red hot and even a small scuttling explosion might trigger off the biggest harbour disaster Malta could know. It was not possible to go aboard to open the sea cocks and explosive charges would have to be placed in the right areas to avoid setting off a violent explosion and at the same time to allow the sea to flood in to counteract the fire and settle the ship.

Volunteers from the cruisers *Aurora* and *Penelope* assembled under Lieutenant Arthur D. Copperwheat, R.N., and, while an intense raid was in progress, the charges were placed in position by Lieutenant Commander Knott. The fuse wire, which it was intended should be laid to an air-raid shelter from which the charges could be detonated, was found to be too short. After it was ensured that all residents had evacuated the area adjoining the harbour, Lieutenant

Copperwheat, lying prone on the shore, joined the wires to complete the electrical circuit. The charges fired and — while all authority held its breath — there was no holocaust. Slowly and safely *Talabot* began to sink and settle. Valletta and the Grand Harbour had been saved. Lieutenant Copperwheat had won the George Cross.

While the intensive battle for the two ships was going on in Grand Harbour, the Luftwaffe was also dividing the defences by strafing the lame, unlucky *Breconshire* in Marsaxlokk Bay. There the Royal Navy had taken on the task of saving what could be saved of the cargo. Officers and ratings were courageously salvaging oil, foodstuffs and war materials in conditions that were filthy, hazardous and under continuous bombardment.

On Friday 27th Royal Marines, Naval ratings and soldiers, including men of the Cheshire Regiment from posts around Grand Harbour, helped the civilian stevedores with the unloading of the two ships now settled in shallow water. They discharged 603 tons from the *Pampas* during the day and 345 tons at night. *Talabot* was still on fire and in such dangerous conditions it was possible to remove only 5 tons. There was still heavy raiding — eight concentrated blitzes by day and two hours of bombing by night. In thus manner the work of salvage went on day after day, for every crate and case of food, every can of kerosene and every box of ammunition was precious. The unloading went on in spite of the continuing fire and the unstable state of some of the cargo. The work was strenuous, dangerous and filthy. Cargo was floating in the holds in water that was thick not only with oil but with condensed milk and other matter from thousands of tins that had burst open. The troops and the stevedores deserved every word of praise bestowed upon them — but not everyone realized the vile conditions in which they were working or the danger to life and limb every time they went below decks to recover the sustenance and warlike materials that the island so badly needed. Many men have earned medals for the kind of bravery shown by so many in this difficult salvage operation. In Malta it was accepted as part of the daily task. The reward? A share of that George Cross earned by joint effort and, after the war, the award to their regiments of the battle honour 'Malta'.

In all, 3,900 tons of cargo were recovered from the 7,462

tons in the holds of *Pampas*, and 1,052 tons from *Talabot* which had been loaded with 8,956 tons. The harbour battle continued over the last nine days of March and extended over Easter into April, when on the 12th *Talabot* was set on fire again. The tense struggle merged and developed into the epic defence of the cruiser *Pepperpot Penelope*—of which we have already read. It was a tough period and the recovery of those thousands of tons of cargo was essential for Malta's survival.

An important lesson was learned, too. In later months when other merchantmen arrived more troops were to be brought in to help unload and they ensured that they were fully organized into distinctive tasks varying from winchmen and hatchwaymen through stevedores to quay stackers and removers. Operations started with the laying of a smokescreen and followed a complete system of dock control, lorry driving and dumping. Hearing that the Tobruk garrison had discharged a record 600 tons in one day, the Malta troops in June 1942 determined to beat it and unloaded 15,000 tons from two vessels in 108 hours. The Hampshires prided themselves on beating all others and in November 1942 working parties from this one battalion alone—while still defending its airfield areas—unloaded 7,785 tons from the *Robin Locksley* in six days. In such manner was morale maintained and survival ensured.

TWELVE

Dobbie Indomitable

His Excellency Lieutenant General Sir William Dobbie was loved by the Maltese. He was a somewhat dour Scot, big in all ways and commandingly capable. A man of distinctive presence, yet apparently humble and obviously God-fearing, he did not seek the limelight nor indulge in propaganda exercises of self-projection. He was deeply religious, a Plymouth Brother, and conducted family prayers after dinner each evening. The Maltese could hardly have contemplated having as a leader a member of a Christian sect so far removed from their own extreme Catholicism — the Brethren being dissenters from the earlier dissenting Anglicans. Yet they appreciated his genuine Christian spirit and approach and his determination to live and act always strictly fairly and without favour. None could sway him from his principles nor his duty. This they knew, acknowledged, understood and respected him for.

As the King's top representative and executive he was accorded the highest regard. The Maltese, who understood these things, and who always demand meticulously correct procedure and precedence for each and every one of their own nobility — and who still proudly recalled that they voluntarily threw in their lot with Britain — gave him full loyalty, trusted his wisdom and accepted his rulings. In an earlier age they would have called him 'Father'. They almost did so in this.

Having been observed, tested, tried and accepted as leader, lord and master, General Dobbie was expected to act as such, untainted and unashamed. He did just that, as a simple, straightforward, understanding, fair and almost regal personage. In his working palace at the seat of government in Valletta, his residential palace at San Anton and his summer palace at Verdala he was unendingly the nearest thing to a king that the island could know, albeit a hard-working, ever-approachable sovereign. Even in the privacy of his residential palace, at least when a guest was living there, his wife, Lady Dobbie, and his daughter Sybil rose whenever he entered a room.

There is no exaggeration in this, odd that it may seem today set down in cold print. When the Hampshires arrived in Malta early in 1941, after settling in and getting to know the people, we felt that we had somehow suddenly slipped back in time; that everything about us was some twenty-five years behind our own known civilization, our thinking and our normal everyday struggle for existence. For one thing there was not the same urgency to achieve and we discovered the "Not to worry, Joe" attitude which in the Maltese produced a happier, easier way of life. Being a maternal society they depended upon direction from above and were almost a feudal nation.

British people found it easy to do 'good works' in Malta. Many women, and men too, who had merely been part of a regiment now developed abilities of compassionate leadership and went forth to organize, help and integrate with the people. This had never happened in India, in Germany with the first British Army of the Rhine, nor in Palestine, nor Egypt. But in Malta the British serviceman and his wife felt respected, admired and wanted. In their associations with the Maltese people many found fulfilment and developed self-expression, were uplifted, encouraged and improved in stature. Maybe this close contact with people of all social classes would not have happened without the war, but it certainly happened during it and quite naturally the top man, Dobbie, was raised to the highest pinnacle.

As a soldier in war and a sapper skilled in defence he was all the more revered and required. When Italy declared war in 1940 and it was obvious that Malta was isolated and vulnerable, General Dobbie's first act as Commander-in-Chief was to issue to the garrison a special Order of the Day. It read:

> The decision of His Majesty's Government to fight until our enemies are defeated will be heard with the greatest satisfaction by all ranks of the Garrison of Malta.
>
> It may be that hard times lie ahead of us, but I know that however hard they may be, the courage and determination of all ranks will not falter, and that with God's help we will maintain the security of this fortress.
>
> I call on all officers and other ranks humbly to seek God's help, and then in reliance on Him to do their duty unflinchingly.
>
> W.G.S.D.

There were already plans for action in case of war and Dobbie must have thoroughly studied them and made his own appreciation. The truth was staggering. This tiny island, 1,000 miles from any friend, was only sixty miles distant and ten minutes' flying time from Sicily. Mussolini immediately roared like a bullfrog threatening to obliterate or capture the island and the Regia Aeronautica came in with the dawn on the first day, attacking within seven and a half hours of the midnight declaration, and made eight terrifying raids that day. The sea and air defences — *Faith*, *Hope* and *Charity* — of Malta have been mentioned elsewhere. The military garrison included only four British infantry battalions, all under strength, and one battalion of the King's Own Malta Regiment, the equivalent of a British Territorial Army unit. The Royal Malta Artillery, a well-trained regular formation, was already manning coastal defences, including some old guns and even primitive bombards. These were early mortars, a hole scooped out of the ground, reinforced with metal, then filled with a hundredweight or so of stones overlaying gunpowder. When fired they could throw their contents a few hundred yards into the sea to inconvenience any vessel close inshore — inefficient and practically useless in World War Two. There were some, but an insufficiency of, anti-aircraft guns.

General Dobbie set about remedying the deficiencies and got guns and men, building up the British battalions eventually to nine — two had left — but it took twenty-one months. He called for conscription, "we fight or perish", a drastic and unpopular measure as in Britain, and the Maltese battalions also built up to match the British — 15,000 of each nationality.

The Maltese individual is not by choice a soldier, although he has qualities of determination and doggedness, a desire to defend his homeland and a capacity to learn. However, he likes to go at his own pace, is unwilling to take command over his friends, and is his own master with no wish to be disciplined to fast, automatic reaction. For Dobbie he undertook to do these things and the martial might increased. There was one other real problem. Every Maltese soldier worried about his family, knowing just where the bombs were falling, and when his home town or village was receiving attention he was doubly anxious. Great tolerance was needed by commanding officers and although it was not possible to grant leave at every whim, some relaxation had to be allowed — especially as so many dwellings were being destroyed and families made homeless. So Dobbie strived and struggled through all the difficulties of transforming a peace-loving people into a nation ready and dedicated to defend to the last. He organized and co-ordinated arrangements for civil defence, air-raid precautions, rehousing and rationing, even to raising a Home Guard. The island was able to put up a stiff resistance and the people demonstrated the will and power to endure. The defensive effort was based mainly on the guns until the Hurricanes arrived. Then on 7 March 1942 Dobbie's first Spitfires breezed in to the nation's delight with their fine superior speed and the ability to take more of the fight to the enemy. It was, therefore, impossible to believe that having been accepted, built up and enshrined in the top power in the hour of desperate need, having received their trust and proved his ability, that he could be, would be, suddenly taken away.

General Dobbie and his family left Malta in the small hours of Friday 8 May 1942. The party left San Anton Palace during the evening of Thursday and went by car to Kalafrana seaplane base, crossing at Birzebugga a tank trap that I knew well. It had temporarily been bridged for the Dobbies but normally it could be negotiated only by a narrow flimsy plank arrangement, in the middle of which I had once ashamedly stalled my motor cycle, effectively halting all others. Some time just after midnight on 7 May Lord Gort arrived by Sunderland flying boat from Gibraltar and the hand-over of governors took place. Then the Dobbies flew off in the same Sunderland for Gibraltar.

The departure of a governor and the arrival of his relief was not a simple matter in a wounded island overlooked by a mass of hostile aircraft waiting to pounce and capture or destroy a most valuable propaganda prize. Secrecy was of the highest priority and it was noteworthy that Gort — presumably deemed the most important, as he was to carry on — was on the island before Dobbie left and the change-over was completed before the islanders knew that any change was imminent.

That is, except for the grapevine. Some people had to know. For example, Dobbie's immediate entourage, whose members were sworn to secrecy. Others knew something unusual was happening. Packing had to be done, files had to be closed, tasks had to be handed over. Unwanted papers, old clothing, pets, had to be disposed of. The Governor, although he would have very much wished to do so, could not speak to the people, but a farewell address was prepared to be delivered next day by a proxy.

Every effort was made to ensure secrecy but there was still a feeling in some quarters that something momentous was about to happen. Two other things were. After the sinking of Vian's deliveries there was again urgent need for food and materials. With as much urgency and secrecy as possible the fast armed and armoured minelayer *Welshman* was being loaded in Britain and being prepared to make a lone rapid run in from Gibraltar. Also, the United States aircraft carrier *Wasp* was being loaded with Spitfires. These would be unarmed, for lightness, and equipped with extra fuel tanks. They would become airborne west of the Sicilian Narrows where they would be met by a Maryland aircraft from Malta and led to the island, thus saving time and also allowing *Wasp* to return quickly to Gibraltar without the necessity to enter the most dangerous area in the Mediterranean.

These things were happening and they came to pass, but meanwhile the grapevine quivered with hints from service, civilian and journalist contacts that the Governor was moving, that he had already left, that his plane had returned, that the Lieutenant Governor had taken over. On 7 May 1942 it seemed certain that Dobbie had gone in a bomber from Luqa, and that his plane after a certain interval had returned to another airfield, probably Hal Far, which is close to Kalafrana.

Francis Gerard was Malta's Information Officer until July 1942 when he left the island. In his book *Malta Magnificent*, published in 1943 before censorship could be lifted on many things, he recounted that the Governor and his family went aboard a bomber at Luqa on 8 May. After a while Dobbie stepped out again and "stood filling his eyes for the last time with the Malta scene". Then he returned to the plane and it was "off on its long journey to England".

Yet the Dobbies certainly left San Anton Palace on the night of 7 May and were waiting at Kalafrana at midnight. Also present was the Luftwaffe which put on a spectacular raid and greeted Gort with a close one as he came ashore from the

Sunderland in Marsaxlokk. Not, of course, because they knew anything about the change-over. Sybil Dobbie recalled the raid in her book *Grace Under Malta*, published in 1944, writing: "Lord Gort arrived in the middle of it. Just as he stepped ashore from the launch a bomb came down so uncomfortably close that a number of people assembled to meet him fell flat on their faces. This apparently oriental form of greeting . . . was a characteristic welcome to Malta." Sybil Dobbie published this in 1944 but the island knew it the day it happened. There were a number of accounts, all mirthful, some malicious, concerning those present. In them all Gort stood unmoved waiting for the proceedings to begin.

Did Dobbie leave twice, from Luqa and from Kalafrana? Was there a dummy run in a bomber—a slow and unheated, uncomfortable way to travel—for deception purposes? In view of the secrecy surrounding his going, why set up a dummy performance? Why put him on view at all when the night motor run to Kalafrana was so easy and unobtrusive? Was there a realization that nothing really could be kept secret and was some elaborate hoax played like the imitation Montgomery at Gibraltar? Was anyone deceived into thinking that Dobbie was still on the island during the daylight hours of 8 May when he was by then already in Gibraltar? Was there a charade played after he left just to cover his homeward flight? I have never discovered the truth but I believe that Dobbie left by Sunderland in the early hours of the 8th. For as secrets could not be kept in Malta, hoaxes could not have been perpetrated successfully—the Maltese would soon have ferreted out a fiction.

Francis Gerard was responsible among other things for a daily situation report of the day's happenings which was issued to the Press. His department also produced a weekly bulletin for the benefit of the public because it was assumed that the *Times of Malta*, with its stablemate the vernacular *Il Berqa*, the only papers still being printed, would slant news in favour of the Constitutional Party as against the Nationalists. This did not happen as far as I could observe. Malta was in dire danger, there was no time nor space for party politics and it was imperative that all pulled together to survive. In the event, the Information Department Weekly Bulletin was itself suspect as a Government-sponsored free propaganda sheet, while the more professional-looking and daily *Times of Malta* at 2*d*. a copy was accepted as the product of working journalists operating in freedom of expression but always seeking the truth. There always is this suspicion of sponsored papers, even when, as with the Bulletin, much effort is made to present truthful reports and to produce articles to give genuine guidance and factual background to the news.

However, Dobbie had gone and there was much speculation as to why he had left when his work had been so worthwhile at a critical time for the island's survival. Was he pushed? Was he ill? Was it deemed necessary to put in a younger man? None of these questions have been satisfactorily answered. However, on 11 May 1942 the God-fearing general was presented to His Majesty the King who invested him with the insignia of the Most Distinguished Order of St Michael and St George. Many rejoiced, but this award was usual for almost any top service in a colony. At the time, superseding the speculation, was the necessity to keep on with the fight.

First let it be recorded that Dobbie's farewell address was duly delivered. In it he declared that he had not been able to say goodbye: "for reasons of high security this was not possible — it was essential that the change of Governor should be known to as few as possible until it was an accomplished fact". He thanked the people for their "great kindness to me" and commended his successor. As well as adjuring them to "put your trust in Almighty God and seek to honour Him in all your ways", Dobbie said:

We have been through stirring times together; times which I will never forget. I am glad that I have had this experience because it has enabled me to get to know and appreciate the people of Malta. I have seen them facing experiences which were so unfamiliar to them, and facing them with the determination and courage of veteran soldiers. I have seen them facing experiences which had become painfully familiar, with the same determination and courage. I have marvelled at the way they have accepted hardships and disasters with cheerfulness, and I consider that the people of Malta have rightly earned the admiration of the whole world — an admiration crystallized in the award of the George Cross to the Island. And now Malta is still facing unprecedented difficulties with the same courage. I am sure that in God's good providence she will in due course emerge out of her difficulties into smoother waters. Until then she will endure and so ensure the final victory.

Yes, Dobbie had seen much suffering and much courage but there was much yet to endure, including lower rations, more and more bombing, and the enervating effects of long years of siege. Now he had gone and a new name that the world knew well flashed through the ether. General the Viscount Gort, V.C., was to lead this indefatigable fortress and a new chapter would open. We knew it meant renewed effort and, we hoped, increased resources. But for a moment we thought of Dobbie flying home. England had been out of our immediate thoughts while our own blitz fermented. Now for a moment, just a moment, we of the garrison imagined again a green and pleasant land in a time of peace.

THOUGHTS OF HOME

I'd like to be on Plymouth Hoe
And watch the coastal steamers go,
Or stand by Cornwall's rocky coast
And hear the seagull's whining boast
Of how he came from far-off France.
Oh, how I long to join the dance
And wander in and out and down
The narrow ways of a Cornish town.

I'd like to taste the clotted cream
At Tavistock beside the stream
And, too, to pick the berries red
That grow in the famous strawberry bed
At Romsey; and at Hayling beach
To laze and watch the children screech
And scramble as they play, until
I fall asleep. And then I'd fill
My dreams with thoughts of Milton Creek,
Of buoys and masts and yachting week.
Of Purbrook Church and Westbrook Grove,
Of boyhood days and fancies wove
About so many childish things,
Like far-off fame and magic rings.

But stay—my frantic fancy runs.
There's work to do. We're manning guns
At half-past four. The Boche will be
For certain dropping 'eggs' for tea.*

Yet I can hear the muffin bell
And smell the buttered toast—Oh hell!
Is Edythe still the cook I knew?
The brown teapot! The goodly brew!

At Petersfield the mellow chime
Of the old church clock! How much I yearn
To see its face; and as I turn
I hear its chaste: 'In time! In time!'
                    In God's good time!

---

* He did. The alarm sounded as I finished writing this line.

THIRTEEN

The Glory of the Tenth

There was little time to think of home, peace and plenty. The first few days after Gort's arrival were hectic and momentous. After the intensive blitz of late March and April the Luftwaffe's raids had eased in intensity though continuing in nuisance value, disorganizing sleep, meals and work patterns. But as soon as the new Governor had arrived early in the morning of Friday 8 May and in the first few days while he was settling in, there was a distinct increase in activity. That day, as the United States carrier *Wasp* was speeding through the Mediterranean towards the island, fighters from Malta destroyed, probably destroyed and badly damaged nine German aircraft, while the guns accounted for another four.

The next day seventy-four unarmed Spitfires from *Wasp* were met west of Pantellaria, led in and landed at Ta'Qali. They took three and three-quarter hours for the journey and began landing around 1 a.m. They jettisoned their auxiliary petrol tanks on the way and had barely twenty gallons in their main tanks on landing—not enough for seeking out a tiny, blacked-out island, nor for evasion had they been attacked. Within six minutes of landing they were armed, ammunitioned, fuelled and ready. It was a miracle of organization. When the Luftwaffe came over, as they had done so many times before, to take their toll on the ground, the new arrivals were already in the air waiting for them. The Germans were surprised and humiliated and lost at least thirty planes that day. The Army had come to the aid of the Royal Air Force and with well-organized and slickly practised routines, with two airmen and two soldiers to each Spitfire, they worked a miracle. Each plane was collected as it landed, led to a pen, refuelled, armed and loaded with ammunition at a speed which amazed the airmen. It amazed the Luftwaffe more.

New arrivals on earlier occasions had not been ready for action for hours, sometimes a whole day. The Luftwaffe from the Sicilian fields only ten minutes' flying time away had found it circumspect not to fight them individually in the air as they flew in but to wait for them to land and then stream in to attempt to destroy them *en masse* on the ground. Usually they had been very successful. This day, under Air Vice Marshal Hugh Lloyd's new policy and the soldier's and airmen's fine co-operative expertise, they were astounded at their reception and the radio waves echoed with guttural cries of *"Achtung! Achtung! Schpitfeuer!"*

Perhaps one of the most expressive comments and appreciative understatements typical of those days was that made by a veteran pilot of Ta'Qali. Within a few minutes of the planes landing he emerged from his dugout and looked skywards where already nearly three squadrons of Spitfires were circling. With a look of awe he exclaimed: "Heavens, look at the fog!"

The next day, Sunday, was to prove greater and more heartening still, going down into the records as the 'Glorious Tenth of May'. At sunrise the fast minelayer *Welshman*, bringing the supplies so vital to the island, completed her unaccompanied 1,000 miles dash from Gibraltar, tied up in Grand Harbour and immediately started unloading the food-stuffs and, especially, ammunition that were so direly needed. She had survived an eventful passage having received attention from E-boats, U-boats, torpedo bombers and dive-bombers until reaching the protective umbrella of Malta Spitfires that had gone out to shepherd her in.

In harbour the Army again was in evidence. A detailed clear-cut plan had been worked out to speed the unloading and to get the stores and warlike materials away from the harbour area quickly. Each man knew his task and those tackling jobs of which they had had no previous knowledge soon mastered the techniques and kept the crates, boxes, sacks and containers moving smoothly and swiftly all day.

First, and for the first time in Malta, a dense smokescreen was laid. Then the troops moved in to effect a well-thought-out unloading operation that continued without rest until the cargo was removed. It was hard, fast, tiring, dangerous work but the servicemen knew the requirement and the deadline. *Welshman* was cleared of oil, food and all stores within five hours. She was able to leave harbour undamaged for the return trip before sundown. The Royal Air Force sent parties to unload their own materials, while four Naval working parties supervised the whole operation aboard ship to relieve *Welshman*'s crew, tired after their hectic passage and with an equally strenuous and dangerous return trip ahead of them through the Sicilian Narrows and back to Gibraltar.

This day's work was a fine performance inspired by the new Governor but it was a hectic period. The Luftwaffe came in greater force than ever—heavy bombers, dive-bombers, fighters, wave upon wave. Only the day-long action of the gunners, with even a better barrage than ever seen before, and the most aggressive fighting by the Royal Air Force, enabled the Army and the dockyard workers to keep to their hard set schedules.

The Luftwaffe did its utmost to sink the minelayer and in its endeavours cast destruction and harassment all around—but paid a bitter price. Bombs exploded all round *Welshman* but they could not hit her. A lorry loaded with meat was blasted into nothingness—except a mass of joints floating in the harbour, which were later retrieved by the dockies. As soon as she was unloaded *Welshman* was moved to another berth. The smokescreen had been maintained but the bombers had been aiming closer; now they were deceived again.

In contrast to earlier actions when the bulk of the defence was necessarily left to the gunners, Lloyd's airmen this time had the new Spitfires to swell their numbers and were able to meet the enemy planes at better odds than had ever before been possible. They waited for them in the sun, swooped to attack the fighters, dropped lower to the heavy bombers and continued right down to take on the Stukas as they were beginning their bombing dives. The screaming Stukas, which sound so frightening with their engines in full throttle and klaxons blaring, are vulnerable with weight as they dive with bombs aboard. They are vulnerable again as they come out of their dive for they pull up with a jerk and the pilot is only half conscious. Many this day were caught by the Spitfires; many went into the sea. Many planes cast their bombs before reaching the island in their efforts to escape and many, so many, were shot down.

One exultant Spitfire pilot reported that the sea between Malta and Sicily was so full of rubber dinghies and shot-down aircraft that it "looked like Henley on Regatta Day". The Luftwaffe lost at least sixty-three planes this day—the

'Glorious Tenth of May'.

Kesselring had about 300 aircraft in Sicily. In seventy-two hours over Malta he lost 112 and there must have been many more damaged. Such losses could not be sustained and quite naturally the bombing of Malta eased considerably. The Italians reported that Kesselring had left Sicily. It was said that his command had been transferred to another front. The Maltese smiled. They knew the true story.

These things all happened as a baptism for the new Governor, and no doubt were influenced by him, too. But the day belonged to the gunners and the airmen, especially the Spitfire pilots, many of whom went right into the flak chasing and destroying the dive-bombers. At least one Spitfire pilot sacrificed his life by this extremely gallant action. A congratulatory message was signalled by the Commander-in-Chief next morning.

It read: "I congratulate all the Fighting Services on their magnificent team work over the weekend and I particularly commend the Royal Air Force and the anti-aircraft defences upon their notable success. The Luftwaffe has seen that wounded Malta can hit back gamely. GORT."

Certainly a full co-operative effort by soldiers, sailors, airmen and civilians, which was what the successful defence and survival of Malta was all about. Like the old-time Musketeers the unspoken but fully carried-out motto was: "Each for all and all for each."

The Air Officer Commanding Malta, Air Vice Marshal Hugh Pughe Lloyd, whose pilots had demonstrated their ability so well over the three days culminating in the 'Glorious Tenth', was soon to receive a knighthood for his part in maintaining over the past momentous year an effective defence of the island and also for building up a fine strike force. This not only harassed Rommel's supply lines but raided inland in Sicily and Italy and into the Aegean. He also kept a watchful eye on the Fleet Air Arm squadrons at Hal Far whose Swordfish biplanes harassed enemy shipping, particularly at night, with torpedoes. He called them his 'Goldfish' and whenever a ship was sunk he presented the successful squadron with a bottle of Plymouth gin—the sailors' favourite; the soldiers' was always Gordons. Spirits of any kind were rare, rationed and highly treasured. Up to the end of 1942 the Fleet

Air Arm squadrons at Malta alone had sunk 400,000 tons of Axis merchant shipping.

Lloyd left on 14 July, being relieved by Air Vice Marshal Sir Keith Park who also was to play a distinguished part with an aggressive strike force. He introduced the system of forward interception as soon as there was a sufficiency of Spitfires to go out to meet the oncoming waves of bombers before they reached the island. During fourteen months on the island Lloyd had worked, lived and slept on the airfields. The idol of his men, to whom he was most approachable, he had demonstrated leadership of the finest quality during a most difficult period. Before leaving the island he told the garrison and the people:

> Malta—this little island . . . enemies on all sides; in splendid isolation—what a nuisance she has been to Italy and Germany. What a thorn in their flesh—and it hurts them grievously. Malta has earned a great name in this war and well does she deserve it—even our foes give her ungrudging admiration. We all know of the campaign in Libya in December 1941 ending with the capture of Benghazi. Malta played a very great part in that campaign. We know the Axis powers were very short of materials of war. Why? Because of Malta, this little island alone in the Mediterranean . . . Malta has every reason to be proud of her part in that campaign and of her contribution to the success of it.
>
> No doubt Rommel told Berlin last winter of his parlous position of supplies. The Germans took a serious view of Malta. If the battle in Africa this year was to run through Egypt and Iraq to Persia, supplies would be required, and they could only be provided by the elimination of Malta as a naval and air base. To make this offensive Germany brought 400 aircraft from her best units in France and Russia and based them in Sicily. Some people say that was a great compliment to Malta, but we would rather not have such compliments. The Germans then staged the most intensive attacks, in the history of air warfare, against this small isolated island. Those 400 aircraft, drawn away from Russia and England, where they might have been doing much damage—their casualty rate over Malta was very high . . .
>
> Yet, in spite of the offensive, in spite of that terrific effort to knock us out, we are stronger in the air today than we have ever been. I suppose our fighter force in this island today, for its size, is the best in the world . . . Malta goes on, undaunted, a bright star in the firmament of the United Nations. We have had a long

climb to where we are today; we have had much hard work and punishment; it has been a momentous struggle. But the top of the hill is not far ahead and Victory may be nearer than we imagine it to be. It has been a great honour to have served with you in our common cause from this small island in the middle of the Mediterranean.

Before he left Lloyd was to understand something of the deep feeling of gratitude the people of Malta had for him when he received a cigarette case sent anonymously by a civilian. It had been inscribed 'M T A P' which, it was explained, there probably being no time to cut the full inscription, meant 'Malta Thanks Air Protection'.

In this same month of July 1942 Viscount Cranbourne, Secretary of State for the Colonies, visited Malta and was greatly impressed, not only by the widespread devastation, but also by the high morale and tenacious spirit of the people. In a broadcast over the Rediffusion system he said:

No one who has visited the island, who has seen what I have already seen, could fail to realize how cruel is the ordeal through which you have passed and are passing. Your cities and towns have been ravaged by bombing; your ancient and beautiful churches and monuments of long and honourable history have been wrecked and blasted; your homes have been reduced to heaps of broken stones.

You have endured all that the malice of the enemy could do against you and you have emerged triumphant and will, I am confident, continue to do so under your gallant Governor, Lord Gort. This I shall be able to tell His Majesty the King and the Prime Minister [Winston Churchill] when I return to England. After two years of siege and bombardment almost unrivalled in history, the defences of Malta remain unbroken and you still carry on your daily life serene and undismayed. Be assured, while you have resisted, the might of the Allies has been gathering. Already its weight is falling in growing measure, by day and by night, upon the enemy. Malta has stood, above all, because the spirit of its people is based on the firmest of all foundations — a deep and abiding trust in God. Throughout your long history that trust has upheld you — and it upholds you now.

On behalf of the Government and people of Great Britain I salute George Cross Malta! God keep you all!

Victory! The hope always for the end of the siege. Just a little further. It was in reality only a few months away but months of further suffering now the food shortage was bringing its own agonizing results with malnutrition and disease. There was need yet for more endurance, more determination. So let us consider the new Governor.

FOURTEEN

Hard Slog

General the Viscount Gort, V.C., arrived in Malta from Gibraltar during the night of 7–8 May 1942 by Sunderland flying boat which set down near Pretty Bay in Marsaxlokk at about midnight. It was quite normal for the slow-flying aircraft to be afforded the added protection of darkness. May 7 was the Vigil of the Feast of Our Lady of Pompeii and the heavy air raid in progress when Gort landed gave the appropriate atmosphere to the day, the man and his mission.

Flashes and roars, hissing, whistling bombs, spluttering shell splinters and shattering, earth-shaking explosions under a canopy of searchlights and streams of arching red tracer shells not only suggested the destruction of Pompeii, but gave appreciative welcome to this well-tried man of war, known for his courage by the cross he wore. And with its thunderous display of light and sound it gave him an immediate indication of his new task.

Lord Gort landed by launch at Kalafrana Fleet Air Arm base and exchanged greetings and confidences with General Dobbie, who with Lady Dobbie and their daughter Sybil then left in the same Sunderland for Gibraltar *en route* to Britain. The new Governor was taken to a partly damaged building where he met the island's civic leaders and Service Commanders. As a bomb exploded barely forty yards away, he was sworn in at a brief though noisy ceremony.

Lord Gort's coming was to herald more intensive attacks. Stricter measures were put in hand to unload swiftly any ship that did manage to get in. Also a system was worked out and practised to move the cargoes quickly and to distribute the contents to small dumps spaced out all over the island. A chain of shaded lanterns was installed on the various routes to assist in guiding the vehicles by night. Some unknown persons, probably afraid that the lights could be seen from the air, removed or doused a number of them during a practice night run. It was, therefore, deemed necessary to broadcast and publish an explanatory notice to reassure the public.

The new Governor showed fine leadership and initiative and his personal courage was demonstrated when he was injured while dealing with a fire at one of the store dumps before the arrival of the fire service. Lord Gort brought with him the George Cross and handed it over to the people. The impressive, solemn, historic but simple ceremony took place in the Palace Square, Valletta, the concourse and balconies being packed to overflowing with the populace. Giving the small silver emblem of their valour into the hands of the Chief Justice, Sir George Borg, for safe-keeping, the Governor and Commander-in-Chief said:

> How you have stood the most concentrated bombing in the history of the world is the admiration of all civilized people . . . The Axis powers have tried again and again to break your spirit, but your confidence in the final triumph of the United Nations remains undimmed. Battle-scarred George Cross Malta stands firm, undaunted and undismayed, waiting for the time when she can call: "Pass, friend, all is well in the Island Fortress!"

In the tense silence as the Governor moved to speak, the battered, pock-marked buildings which had themselves borne witness to so much heroism and suffering seemed in their drab war covering of bomb-dust and scars to be listening for the next bomber raid — but nothing disturbed the ceremony. One phrase in Lord Gort's speech deserves to be emphasized here: "the most concentrated bombing in the history of the world . . ." Whatever else is forgotten, and much will be, this fact must be remembered, and also that their agony was continuous, day after day, night after night, week after week, month after month, even — if this fact can be appreciated — year after year! Day after day for year after year!

The Cross, guarded by two sentries, was placed on view in the Palace Square in front of the Main Guard. The people filed by to examine and admire it. After some days it was taken and exhibited in each village in turn. In this way the whole nation was able to file by and inspect the tiny, shining silver symbol that reflected their exploits in the Great Siege they were still enduring. They knew then that they were living the history that would long be recounted proudly in the centuries to come.

IN THE ISLAND OF THE CROSS

*"Guarded by two sentries . . . the Decoration was
then left for the people to file by and inspect . . ."*

Even the suckling was there at the seeing,
Laughing and gurgling, then clutching her breast;
While on to her skirts clung the toddler conceiving
The light in her eyes — and the multitude prest.

Even the sick and the lame were about her,
Even the aged and the bride and the groom.
In the 'Black Winter' the world did not doubt her,
And now for the whole world she edged and made room.

Her troubles, her sorrows, the loss of her childer!
Little left and yet still undistressed, undismayed,
She held her head high. Oh they could not bewilder
The light in her eyes — there her cross lay displayed.

Lord Gort toured the island, met the people, surveyed
the damage and soon understood the tremendous task ahead
of him. He set to work with determination, but it would be
another two years before the nation would know, even semi-
officially, how near this month of May was to surrender.
Perhaps it was merciful, too, that they did not know of the
long, hard months still ahead. It was not until March 1944,
after the siege was raised, when the Allies were making very
slow progress fighting northward in Italy, that John Gordon,
Editor of the *Sunday Express*, revealed something of the
desperate situation in Malta on Gort's arrival.

Counselling against the pessimistic attitude that some in
Britain were voicing about the slowness of the advance in
Italy, Gordon wrote in exhortation:

When Lord Gort, then Governor of Gibraltar, was ordered
suddenly one day to proceed to Malta and take over the
Governorship of the island, he was told that the island was
unlikely to be able to hold out for more than another six weeks
and that his task would probably be to make the capitulation. It
was, perhaps, the grimmest, hardest duty ever set that brave and
grand man.

He flew to Malta during the night, landed in conditions of some peril, and was sworn in during a heavy air raid. "That night," he said to me, "I resolved that rather than capitulate by formal surrender, if the crisis came, I would lead what remained of the garrison in an invasion of the coast of Italy and go down fighting."

In the morning he looked round his island and summed up its prospects. He had very few planes, a very small garrison and very empty stores, both of food and munitions. But he had behind him a fighting people. He decided that he still had a chance. And he decided to take the chance. He had more planes brought in although at a terrible cost. The Navy got his vital convoy through just by the skin of its teeth. He tackled the food situation with such success that he swung the island off the razor edge of starvation.

And Malta did not surrender. It survived to see Italy fall.

Had Lord Gort decided to set sail for Italy and 'go down fighting' it is certain that he would have taken an enthusiastic, determined garrison with him. The troops, especially the infantry who could not fight back at the bombers, were madly frustrated at being unable to reply and many volunteered for any kind of aggressive action. Apart from fully supporting the Royal Air Force on the ground, which was already being done, the only fighting possibility seemed to be as crewmen on aircraft. This, however, is a specialized job and in any case there were more trained personnel than planes. So the P.B.I. just soldiered on.

It was because of this frustration and the boredom of repetitive tasks, coupled with the continuous concentrated bombing on and around military targets which did in some cases set nerves a-jangling, that the Command Fair had been set up under Dobbie's administration. In the conditions then prevailing the ordinary private soldier had little freedom of movement. Officers had the power and need to move around their commands and beyond them in liaison duties. Non-commissioned officers, too, could move around their own sectors, but the individual Tommy could have only one task—to fire upwards if he had a Bren gun or to keep his head down if he had not.

This, of course, in his defensive position. His other jobs, such as aiding the Royal Air Force, stevedoring, repairing, clearing and constructing airfields and aircraft pens, did give some movement and the feeling of assisting the communal effort, but they kept him everlastingly in the target area and he did need some break at times.

Two captains, Ken Crossley on the General List, assisted by Bill Taylor of the Manchesters, were given the task of setting up a 'relaxation' centre. In spite of being in the harbour target area the Command Fair opened in the old police barracks near Fort St Elmo in Valletta and included the Long Ward of the old Hospital of the Knights, said to be the largest unsupported hall in Europe. Here in 1943 Montgomery was to 'put in the picture' all officers of the Malta garrison, 'no exemptions', immediately before the invasion of Sicily. As he started his speech with: "Cigarettes out! Cough!" we wondered if the one bomb that could cast all Malta's and Monty's leadership into oblivion would fall. It did not. I do not think that we were fearful or bomb-happy, merely used to being more cautious and careful in our knowledge than visitors ever seemed to be initially.

The Command Fair opened a bar of sorts and set up side shows almost like an English fair or amusement arcade, but chiefly it got troops together under one roof with weekly entertainments and sing-songs. They called the show the P.B.I. Parade and it was also broadcast over the Rediffusion system. No ENSA concert party could reach besieged Malta but Ken and Bill devised some spectaculars to entertain the troops and give them that little spot of normality and relaxation they so badly needed. The troupes that formed and helped to entertain included the Raffians and the Whizz Bangs. The former was made up of airmen and their wives, while the latter was a travelling English concert party that had been unable to leave Malta when war struck. Ken Crossley also sought out local talent which thoroughly encouraged the troops.

As Education Officer of the Hampshires I was told by my commanding officer to organize something of interest to get the troops thinking of things other than the safety factors of a slit trench and the abnormally high number of bombs attracted to the battalion area. Lectures never succeeded in a target area when ears and minds were attuned for instant action. Illustrated talks with an epidiascope failed in barely suppressed laughter through the lack of electricity at the vital moment. However, in January 1942 after the Hampshires had been on the island for a year, and some fourteen months before they left for Egypt to prepare for the invasion of Sicily, I did manage what was considered to be impossible—to get the whole battalion together for an afternoon.

Booking the United Services' Club, Valletta, for half a day, and leaving as few as practicable to maintain the defences, we defied all hazards, including the Luftwaffe, and proceeded to enjoy an all-ranks afternoon dance. The four hours' break enabled the unit to assemble in relaxed comradeship—the first time we had been together under one roof for over four years. In the interim we had been in India, Palestine, the Canal Zone and the Matruh area of North Africa, with some participation in Wavell's first explosive advance. From 1938 the battalion had always been widely dispersed. Now in Valletta the Cheshire Regiment provided a dance band and Ken Crossley by great efforts produced a Command Fair cabaret of delightful originality. The inexperience and inadequate rehearsal of a chorus line of charming high-kicking local young ladies only added to the hilarity and appreciation. The troops had found something different to laugh about, for a few hours had new surroundings and a relaxation from watchful readiness. They went back to their same old tasks but feeling a mite refreshed.

Many attempts were made to get convoys through from Britain and Gibraltar in the west and from Alexandria in the east. Some vessels did get to harbour but many were sunk *en route*, some were forced to turn back and, most tragically disappointing of all, some were destroyed and sunk in harbour. The use of troops as stevedores to supplement the dockies and the wise inclusion of dehydrated foods, which compacted more sustenance into less space, helped to stave off defeat. As also did the swift movement of the cargoes from docks to the widely dispersed dumps, even at night during raids and black-out.

Every ship that came in brought hope to the population who each time eagerly awaited an announcement that rations would be increased. Alas, no one knew when the next ship would get through, nor if any would, and it was therefore imperative that new stocks be firmly husbanded. Time and time again, each after a long interval, the Maltese were disappointed when the hope of extra food had run high, and time and time again they philosophically adjusted their belts, boring more and more holes to ease the ache.

The 29 May 1942 was the thousandth day of war between Britain and Germany since the declaration on 3 September 1939. For Malta it was the 719th day of repeated attacks since Italy had entered on 10 June 1940. The month of May brought the 2,000th air raid. For nearly two years there had been raids at the rate of nearly three a day—day after day, night after night. All normal routine was interrupted, intentionally, by the enemy. There was usually a raid at mealtimes, morning, midday, evening; while at night, even when there were no heavy raids, someone somewhere was being bombed or perhaps a lone marauder would search and fly around for hours.

Often there would be intensive action, but always there were sleep-disturbing, routine-upsetting alerts. Work still continued, interrupted by raids, schools were still attended as and when possible; while in the forces offensive training was carried out in spite of the defensive nature of the present task and the immense amount of unusual activity that was necessary, such as crater filling, stevedoring, airstrip making and aircraft refuelling and rearming. The civilians doggedly accepted the upset of routine, made what they could of the rationed food and strove to remain alive. This was a time for stamina and determination, a time to endure, but it was not the end. There must be a turning point and there was still faith that it could and would be reached.

ONE THOUSAND DAYS

One thousand days have died O God,
And passed are twice one thousand raids.
The Hun may wield his bloody rod,
Our faith in Thee dims not nor fades.
  O God of Courage, Hope and Right,
  Maintain us steadfast in this fight.

One thousand days of blasting war,
Yet still Thy tireless, steadfast host,
Unconquered, sleepless, bloody, sore,
Defy the tyrant Hun to boast.
  O God of Courage, Hope and Right,
  Maintain us steadfast in this fight.

Two thousand raids long since have passed,
But still the rock stands firm and grim.
The Rock of Faith-in-Thee at last
Shall triumph o'er their pagan hymn.
O God of Courage, Hope and Right,
Maintain us steadfast in this fight.

Four-square we meet the heathen band,
Each in his drilled and practised part;
Civilian, soldier, sailor stand
With fearless airman, stern of heart.
O God of Courage, Hope and Right,
Maintain us steadfast in this fight.

The martyr nations wait Thy sign;
Free loving peoples watch the sky.
We stand *en masse* — no single line —
Thy cross our symbol; this our cry:
O God of Courage, Hope and Right,
Maintain us steadfast in this fight.

In June 1942 after Lord Gort had specially signalled for aid, a large operation was laid on to restock the island. Two convoys were to converge simultaneously from east and west. Sadly, of eleven merchant ships from Alexandria and six from Gibraltar, only two in the latter convoy reached Malta, but these two were gratefully received.

The Alexandria convoy ran up against an Italian–German force and the merchantmen were ordered back to save the cargoes, while the escort fought a tough engagement in which there were losses on both sides. The Mediterranean Fleet lost one light cruiser, four destroyers and two escort vessels sunk and thirty aircraft shot down, while the Italian losses were one eight-inch gun cruiser, two destroyers and one U-boat sunk. The Luftwaffe lost at least sixty-five aircraft. Such was the heavy cost of attempting to succour Malta even when no supplies got through.

We know now from German sources that the increased Axis activity directed at Malta in May and June 1942 was the overture of an attempt to eliminate the island whose warships and aircraft were seriously depleting the supplies running south from Italy to North Africa. Rommel, who was then advancing eastward south of Gazala, was given authority to attack Tobruk but was ordered by the German High Command to halt at the Egyptian frontier to allow the fullest concentration to be directed at Malta. The island was to be 'taken out' — it was too great a hindrance between North Africa and Italy.

Thus Malta's aggressive activity and the people's ordeal were directly linked to the respite the troops in the field might experience, although neither private soldier in North Africa nor civilian in Malta could know how closely their efforts were connected. Both were also tightly bound with the ratings on warships and the submariners and airmen hunting and strafing the Axis convoys. However, when Tobruk was taken with its essential harbour on 21 June and 8th Army was escaping eastward, the neutralization of Malta was called off to enable Rommel to try to overtake and destroy the British in the field.

Rommel, then elated by success, knew that he had the initiative and believed that the destruction of 8th Army was possible and preferable to the elimination of Malta. An Austrian conscript with the German Army, Paul Hofmann, who happened to be a journalist and who later escaped to the British, told of an evening at Rommel's headquarters in the Libyan desert when a row broke out between the 'Desert Fox' and Kesselring, German Supreme Commander South, who was on a visit from Sicily. Rommel was boasting that he could reach the Nile and was selecting from a brochure the personal suite he would occupy in the famous British rendezvous, Shepheard's Hotel in Cairo. Amid much heat that generated into an animosity that was never thereafter quenched, Kesselring stormed: "You play with fire. You risk everything if you try to reach the Nile while the British still hold Malta." Rommel got his way and resumed the chase of 8th Army. The attack on Malta eased. The island was not 'taken out' — but 8th Army got away.

One effect of the strikes by Malta-based aircraft, submarines and surface warships on convoys from Sicily to North Africa was that Axis shipping perforce preferred to take the shortest route and the Italian navy had no heart nor inclination to sail the longer distances to ports just behind Rommel's front line and thus ease his logistic problems, which were considerable. This also meant that much more fuel was required to get supplies forward from Tripoli, 500, 1,000 or more miles from the front. Also there were times when some units in the field were without fuel for vehicles and when heavy artillery in Tripoli could not move forward because of the lack of petrol.

In 1941 Tobruk had been spared an air bombardment because Hitler gave a direct order that the Luftwaffe should protect merchantship convoys whose losses were running extremely high, even as much as 50 per cent of the shipping being destroyed by Malta-based aircraft and the Royal Navy.

In the autumn of 1942, that is in the three critical months before Alamein, the total number of ships available to the Axis forces was only four fast and seven slow transports, which confined Rommel's supply line to a mere two or three ships a week.

But to get back to the June convoys and Gort's reaction. The new Governor broadcast to the nation on 16 June 1942, the day that seventeen ships were due but only two got in. In a long talk he took the people into his confidence with regard to the supply position and the need to conserve. He also advised against Black Market activities and warned against Fifth Column thinking. He said, among other things:

> The truth never hurts . . . we are always at our best when we know the worst . . . Let us remember that the most glorious sieges in history have always meant hardships, and without hardships there would be little glory. Malta has shown to the world that she can endure and the world knows that Malta will never weaken . . . Hard work lies ahead of us; our harvest is vital and we must make all possible savings in every commodity and stock. Let us always pause to think whether we can make some saving and some sacrifice every day . . . We have the conviction that our cause is just, we have trust in ourselves and we have a still greater belief in our faith in Almighty God. Strong in that faith let us go forward together to victory.

When Lord Gort had made his preliminary tour of assessment around the island he came to the village of Marsaxlokk on the south-east coast and situated at the head of the wide and deep bay of the same name. Some of us who had studied the problem from the enemy angle and had written appreciations of the possible invasion pattern had concluded that

Marsaxlokk was the most likely initial landing area. Gort apparently thought this way, too, for he told the villagers that they could be right in the way of a seaborne invasion and might be well advised to move inland while they still had the freedom to organize their evacuation and rehousing. This was not defeatist philosophy, for as already recorded Gort was thinking aggressively. It was prudent caution, consideration for the inhabitants and part of his policy of taking the people into his confidence. In the event the humble fisherfolk stayed put.

Four days after Gort's broadcast the Lieutenant Governor, Sir Edward Jackson, also spoke to the nation, giving more details of the measures to be taken for survival. In his address he said:

> Our security depends, more than anything else, on the time for which our bread will last. I am not now speaking of our power to resist invasion or to resist bombing from the air. We believe we can repel invasion and we know that we can resist bombing. We have proved that to the enemy and to the world. That is why the enemy is trying to beat us by the only means left. He is trying to starve us out and there is reason to believe that he is a good deal puzzled by the fact that he has not already done so . . .
>
> Bread is our main food . . . what we have is our own and we intend to keep it and share it equally among us all . . . you will understand that when a ration is reduced or a wider interval made between the dates of issue the object is to make things last, wherever possible, so long as bread will last . . . England will not forget us and the Royal Navy and the Royal Air Force will see us through . . . If we are to make our present stocks last to the Target Date we can issue the present ration only once in every two weeks instead of once a week.

So at one stroke the ration was halved, but the people knew that there was no other way to survival of their own long-cherished way of life. They shrugged their shoulders, grumbled of course, said "*Allura!* Not to worry!" and settled again to the old routine with grim determination. But not before a number had spontaneously gathered beneath the windows of the Jackson villa and with accordions and guitars serenaded the old so-and-so. Just to demonstrate their understanding.

The Royal Navy and the Royal Air Force were still aggressive and continued to strike at the Afrika Korps and at the ships endeavouring to get supplies across to Rommel from Sicily and the Italian mainland. Torpedo-carrying Swordfish biplanes and heavy Wellington bombers were flying out nightly and it was sad to note their dwindling numbers as the latter were gradually reduced to six, five, four . . . And the more effective the British actions, the harder the Luftwaffe struck back at the island.

FIFTEEN

Convoy Courageous

'Can you see the stuff they're piling on the quay?
Can you see the price that's written? (P'raps you can't decipher it.)
It was paid for twice, thrice over as they brought it through the sea.'

Forty convoys of merchantmen sailed to Malta during the siege, eight of them from Britain. It takes a lot of food to keep an island of nearly 300,000 people alive. It takes a lot of shells, small arms ammunition, gun replacements and aircraft parts just to keep it defensive. When that island — that the Italians were the first to call "that unsinkable aircraft carrier" — is also aggressive, it needs an immense amount of high octane petrol for aircraft and fuel oil for warships in addition to steel, cement, timber, coal and many hundreds of warlike and mundane articles down to rivets, screws and nails.

The population needed wheat for bread, but man does not live by bread alone, as the Maltese soon discovered. The food that had to be brought in included maize, rice, beans, coffee, salt, fats, onions, frozen and tinned meat, peanuts, milk, even eggs. For the greater ease of handling, storing and refuelling aircraft much of the aviation spirit came in four-gallon cans and there were also medical stores, tobacco, spirits, cigarettes, soaps, cloth, cars, guns and spare barrels, lorries, forage for goats and the few horses. Hundreds of miscellaneous articles were needed from needles to novels; not forgetting, of course, babies' napkins, dummies and bottles. It takes a lot of many things to keep a nation alive and it needs little imagination on the part of the enemy to understand the stranglehold that can be exerted on an aggressive island isolated a thousand miles from help.

Forty convoys sailed to Malta but many ships never completed the voyage. During the six months to August 1942 out of forty vessels sailing from Britain fifteen were lost. In that period 43 per cent of the 314,690 tons shipped from the United Kingdom did not arrive, while 34 per cent of the 296,000 tons sent from Egypt disappeared beneath the waves.

These are heavy losses, not only in badly needed stores, but in highly prized, almost irreplaceable ships and, most sad of all, in brave, hard-trained, dedicated men. Like the airmen who flew in defence of the island, knowing every time they took off that the odds of survival were against them, the merchant seamen also knew deep in their hearts that at least one ship in three would not survive that last hectic dash through the Sicilian narrows where mines as well as submarines, E-boats and dive-bombers took their toll while many of the surface escort were busily chasing Italian warships. The incredibly brave seamen who time and again worked the merchantmen through knew that they could only expect to survive two voyages out of three.

At times the odds were even greater. Convoys had to turn back. Others lost all ships. Like the March 1942 sailing from Alexandria which almost got through intact but then suffered one ship sunk and sadly had the other three bombed to the bottom in harbour—heartbreaking and demoralizing after completing the hazardous, exhausting voyage. Yet there were always merchant sailors ready to try once again to bring relief to the stricken isle.

The people of Malta knew the hazards that beset them and praised their tenacity and courage. They, too, were suffering and they understood the urge and the agony, the driving force and the faith that encouraged them and brought them through. Merchant seamen have remarked that the bastions around Grand Harbour—Europe's largest natural anchorage and shelter—were "built as though fashioned for greeting" and the Maltese used them and filled them and cheered the ships in. Even at night they stood on the bastions and the harbour echoed their gratitude—an exciting dramatic welcome to battle-scarred, fatigue-ridden mariners at the end of a long, hard run.

Without the Royal Navy the convoys could never have lived through the long, hazardous voyages. The slower merchantmen were easy prey to submarines, surface craft and aircraft, but the discipline of the convoy, as well as the armament, and the speed of the white ensign escort, gave protection to many that might have straggled and then struggled against impossible odds. The Royal Navy gave advice and chivvied and chased and cherished their charges but the merchant seamen, especially the master, is his own man with his own special responsibilities to his ship, his crew and his owners. In the end the white ensign and the red duster worked well together, realizing that the safety of the whole must supersede the good of the individual.

The Admiral gave the orders, or instructions, and Royal Navy liaison officers and signallers aboard the merchantmen helped to interpret them. The cruisers and destroyers moved up and down the lines keeping the ships in station, cajolling and encouraging, urging them on when necessary and keeping watch and guard. Typical of the instructions were those issued from the battleship *Renown* by Vice Admiral Sir James Somerville to the convoy of July 1941. His message to each master after leaving Gibraltar read: "Remember, everyone, that the watchword is: THE CONVOY MUST GO THROUGH." He prefaced this as follows:

> For over twelve months Malta has resisted all attacks of the enemy. The gallantry displayed by the garrison and people of Malta has aroused admiration throughout the world. To enable this defence to be continued it is essential that your ships, with their valuable cargoes, should arrive safely in the Grand Harbour.

There followed the exhortation and then details about keeping signal lights dim even by day, all other lights out, even navigation lights, no smoke, keeping station and keeping going if damaged.

Because of the dangers of the passage and the uncertainty of arrival—one might almost say the certainty of some non-arrivals—the cargoes on ships bound for Malta were always fully mixed so that no matter how many or how few ships arrived there was always some ammunition, some meat, some cloth, something of many things. The diversity was the result of experience, hard learned when a vital shipment of coal was lost in 1941 and from well-remembered disastrous cargoes to Egypt in World War One. But this distinctive loading made secrecy more difficult, made it hard to disguise the destination of ships so laden. The dockies' jargon "loaded Malta cargo" became the spies' interpretation "Malta bound".

Certainly there was leakage of destination information. It was reported that crates marked 'Malta' were plainly visible on the quayside of a British port. Questions were asked in

Parliament after the August 1942 convoy, which was vital, heavily protected and yet lost nine out of fourteen ships sunk, the others damaged. The tanker *Ohio*, twice evacuated, was literally 'carried' into port, the Royal Navy suffered grievous loss and many fine, courageous seamen have 'Malta convoy' as their honoured epitaph.

Although such operations were fully secret the Maltese people were talking about a 'big convoy' even before the ships left Britain and were forecasting the arrival as mid-August. It was said that the Italians also knew and in a broadcast directed at Malta declared they would ensure it never arrived. Rumours are rife in times of stress, wishful thinking can enlarge tiny truths. Everyone knew that relief was necessary, that there must be some endeavour to break through. So fact and fancy perhaps combined to give life and body to what was originally hopeful thinking and in the end turned out to be true. Such, perhaps, is the substance of faith and hope that carries the spirit expectantly through to the strength of the glorious tomorrow that must always eventually dawn.

Nevertheless, in spite of what was supposed to be strict secrecy in Britain and Malta many people on the island knew that some ships were on the way and roughly when to expect them. The impossibility of keeping a secret was noticeable throughout the siege and despite being cut off from the outside world happenings in England often seemed to be known simultaneously on the island. Secrets are not broadcast by radio and, indeed, there were few receiving sets in Malta and no electricity for many months. Yet, somehow, the Maltese always knew.

So in August 1942 the biggest convoy yet assembled sailed from Britain in what was intended to be the vital relieving operation. Fourteen merchantmen were loaded in England and with a large escort of warships and carriers sailed past Gibraltar to attempt the 1,000 miles run to the island against enemy surface vessels, including fast speeding E-boats, submarines, Junkers 88, Stuka dive-bombers, fighters and torpedo-carrying planes; not forgetting the minefields and mines parachuted into the path of the convoy. The escort included three admirals, three aircraft carriers with their planes, two battleships, seven cruisers and twenty-four destroyers. A large armada for a large task. Churchill had answered Gort's call and was determined that Malta should be relieved. The Axis was equally emphatic that the effort should fail.

Incidentally, this convoy was numbered WS21S — WS signifying it was one of 'Winston's Specials', which normally sailed to Egypt round the Cape of Good Hope. So obviously there was some attempt at deception of the enemy.

On reaching Gibraltar some smaller naval vessels called in as they needed to refuel and on Sunday 9 August religious services were held aboard the fleet seeking divine help and guidance during the perilous passage ahead. A BBC naval commentator later broadcast that at the end of the simple service 'God Save The King' was sung with such great enthusiasm "as I have never heard it sung before".

The convoy was already 100 miles into the Mediterranean when dawn broke on the Monday and Vice Admiral E. N. Syfret, commanding the operation, sent this signal from his flagship, the battleship *Nelson*, to every vessel in the convoy:

> The garrison and people of Malta, who have been defending their island so gallantly against incessant attacks by the German and Italian air forces, are in urgent need of replenishments of food and military supplies. These we are taking to them and I know that every officer and man in the convoy and its escort will do his utmost to ensure that they reach Malta safely.
>
> We may be sure that the enemy will do all in his power to prevent the convoy getting through and it will require every exertion on our part to see that he fails in his attempt. During the next few days all ships will be in the first and second degrees of readiness for long periods. When you are on watch be especially vigilant and alert and, for that reason, when you are off duty get all the sleep you can. Every one of us must give of his best. Malta looks to us for help. We shall not fail them.

The first day's sailing eastward was uneventful, calm over blue waters under a brilliant sun. But all watched keenly and waited tensely knowing that the test would come, for under these waters lay the carrier *Ark Royal*, an early victim of the war. The night passed and Tuesday noon. Then with shattering suddenness at 1.24 p.m. came a violent explosion dramatically announcing the hidden enemy's presence. Three more echoing booms in quick succession from a submarine's salvo of torpedoes turned the aircraft carrier *Eagle* over, sent her planes sliding and her crew into the sea. They saved 950 officers and men and a destroyer raced them back to Gibraltar. The *Eagle* in her time had been a great benefactor to Malta.

Among the survivors from the carrier was Reuter's special correspondent Norman Thorpe whose despatch, telegraphed later to London from Gibraltar, described the last moments of the ship before she slipped below the waves to join her sister *Ark Royal*. He wrote of four explosions which "rocked the ship" and of how he eventually scrambled up to the upper deck with the vessel listing "terrifyingly on the port side". He had only partially blown up his lifebelt when, with the deck "slanting more sharply than a gabled roof", he slid down into the choppy sea. Having got clear of the ship and with every wave washing over his head, he could see *Eagle* lying on her side while, "down the great red expanse of her underside men were sliding into the sea". There were six or seven explosions from depth charges dropped by a destroyer hunting the U-boat and then "a mighty rumbling" as the sea-water poured in and forced the air out of *Eagle*. Thorpe was picked up almost immediately and so were most of the officers and ratings. Later, aboard the rescuing destroyer, Captain L. D. MacKintosh, commanding *Eagle*, said to him: "How marvellously cool the officers and men behaved. I saw no sign of panic in the last few minutes of the life of the ship."

The convoy sailed on amid the noise and disturbance of depth charges being dropped by destroyers hunting six separate U-boats now known to be in the vicinity of the merchantmen. Then came the Junkers 88 bombers and the Italian torpedo-carrying planes and the fight for survival began. For five hours the ships pressed forward, putting up a barrage that prevented any enemy aircraft from registering even one direct hit, while the planes from the carriers went out to meet the formations and fight them at distance. Those that got through they chased and harassed. The night brought respite from bombing but no time to relax watchfulness, for E-boats and U-boats were now the danger and there was all the more need to keep in station—a protective horseshoe formation with its opening to the rear.

On the Wednesday, through the deluge of bombs and torpedoes, through the haze of smoke and spray, and with mines being parachuted ahead of them, they fought their way on-ward and the first of the merchantmen faltered and failed. Damaged by near misses and hit by a torpedo, she slowly sank exhausted by effort. That evening a shattering, flashing explosion signalled the end of the task for the cruiser *Nigeria*, flagship of Rear Admiral H. M. Burrough, supervising cruisers and destroyers. He transferred to the destroyer *Ashanti* to continue to Malta, while the crippled *Nigeria* returned westward to Gibraltar for repairs. There were poignant moments when the crew volunteered to accompany the Admiral but he reminded them that their duty was to get the ship back into service whilst his was to proceed with the convoy.

The Stuka dive-bombers came that evening, too, and proved more accurate than the 88s. The enemy 'first eleven', the seamen called them. A merchantman was hit and the cruiser *Cairo* sunk, while after dark E-boats were discovered assembling to attack and had to be fought off. During this disastrous night several merchantmen were damaged and the cruiser *Manchester* and the destroyer *Foresight* were so badly crippled that it was deemed advisable to sink them. Two merchantmen were lost.

As this is a book on the people of Malta it is not the place to recount the many stories of this most harassed and heroic convoy, but such closely connected events did obviously influ-ence feeling on the island and the tales of heroism, dedication to duty and danger overcome gave added boost to morale. The story of the merchantman *Brisbane Star* is typical of the deter-mination to get through and of the bravery of officers and men when the direst menace strikes and the ship has to fight alone or founder. It shows, too, the canny cunning quality of the British seaman that was necessary to outwit adversaries who held all the aces.

The *Brisbane Star* fell out of the convoy when a torpedo opened her bows. The master, Captain Riley, knew that he had just one chance. He made straight for the neutrality of French territorial waters off North Africa. There he literally played bluff with a German submarine which dogged him at periscope depth, and an Italian plane which followed the ship and flew tantalizingly low enough to offer a fair target. Any belligerency would have violated international law and be plainly visible to thousands of potential witnesses watching on shore. The game of 'attack if you dare' went on for five long hours with the submarine following close enough to be shot at and the plane repeatedly swooping low enough to be blasted out of the sky. The *Star* sailed back and forth but never left the sanctuary of French coastal waters.

The plane left to refuel, the U-boat dived to rest knowing that dusk would not fall until 8 p.m. and the *Star* could not dare to leave before that hour as it would be a sitting target in open waters. Captain Riley knew all these hazards and understood how his adversary would react, so at 6 p.m.—two hours before dusk—he turned on full steam and made a dash for Malta hoping that the U-boat commander would still wait for dusk. He did. Captain Riley had judged his adversary aright. The *Brisbane Star* sailed unmolested through the night and eventually reached the island, but not before the same Italian plane found her next morning and dived to attack.

Now she was in open waters and the ship's gunners, commanded by an army officer, aimed and waited patiently for the last split second before they fired. They made no mistake. It was the plane that died. The *Brisbane Star* sailed into Grand Harbour a day after the main convoy. Only the cunning of her skipper, the brave, stoic co-operation of her crew and the patient, deadly accuracy of her gunners had saved her valuable cargo. The Maltese knew she might have been interned but had preferred to get there the hard way and they fully and volubly applauded.

For the remainder of the convoy the epic voyage had continued. The aerial attacks were vicious and continuous. Both submarines and E-boats were active, ever-present menaces. The mines in set fields and parachuted into the open sea made the going more perilous in the fog and noise of battle, with smoke and flame and high-flying spray from near misses making observation that much more difficult. So the convoy steamed on, but this day six more merchantmen were lost.

When dawn broke on Thursday 13th the few surviving indomitable merchant vessels of the convoy had passed through the Sicilian narrows but had still another full day's sailing to complete. If all went well they might reach harbour by nightfall. The large Royal Navy escort turned back to

Hanging out the washing from a window above one of
Valletta's streets

A temporary shopping area in 'The Ditch' near Floriana

Delivering the milk in a Valletta street, direct from goat to housewife

Shopping queue in Zachary Street, Valletta

The paraffin man by the Auberge de Castille (Army headquarters), Valletta

Paraffin queue during an air-raid alert

A family in their cave home in 'The Ditch'

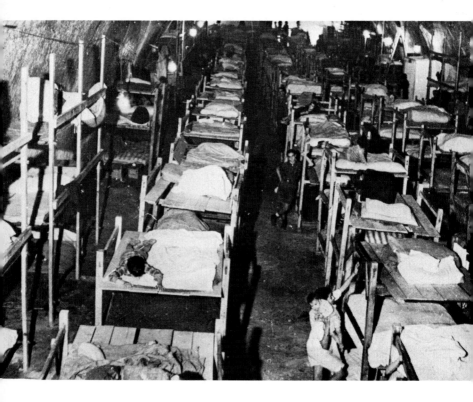

Hundreds slept underground in Valletta

Washing clothes out of doors. In blitzed houses, the family had to live in one room

Prayers in a shelter

Children at play, 1942

Maltese children

Scout Peter Parker doing telephone picket on the docks

A miniature flag station set up
under the high bastions of
Valletta

Children celebrate the fall of Tripoli, waving flags begged and
borrowed from shops and churches

General Dobbie, Governor of Malta, in Valletta, standing, in khaki peaked cap, behind marine

Field Marshal 'Tiger' Gort was accorded the adulation of a hero's departure before leaving the island on relinquishing the governorship. He was driven through Kingsway, Valletta, on 5 August 1944, accompanied by cheering crowds

'The Captain' (left) in 19 at Safi airstrip with Company Sergeant Major Jim Burgess of the Hampshir Regiment

Gibraltar, though some destroyers remained, and an umbrella of Malta Spitfires and Beaufighters took over to stand guard and to fight off intruders during the last few score miles. The coast of Sicily was barely fifty or sixty miles to the north of the convoy route and enemy fighters were now within range to augment the bombers and to harass the ships and their escort. Moreover, it was still necessary to avoid minefields and to watch for floating mines and the menace of U-boats and E-boats that might at any time emerge from their rock cavern hide-outs on Pantellaria. The ships' gunners still had a hectic time fighting off aerial attacks.

In Malta we now knew quite definitely that the convoy was coming, although the only visible manifestation was the hectic activity around the airfields where, like a swarm of buzzing, bustling, hard-flying, almost angry, bees fighter planes were continuously rushing in from the west to touch down immediately, rearm and refuel, and then speed westward again. We knew that a carrier had been lost but censorship forbade mention of the name. Yet Norman Thorpe's report was at this critical time being beamed by Reuter to world recipients. Even in Southern Rhodesia, for example, *The Bulawayo Chronicle* was setting up the type announcing *Eagle*'s destruction while Malta was observing silence and the Royal Navy and the Royal Air Force were doing their utmost to get what remained of the convoy through.

A special German announcement this day claimed not only the sinking of *Eagle* but also heavy damage to the carrier *Furious* "which entered Gibraltar with a heavy list", and the setting on fire of the United States carrier *Wasp* "after six direct bomb hits". The Germans claimed the sinking of "nine merchant ships totalling 90,000 tons" and damage to "three cruisers and six large merchantmen and tankers totalling 50,000 tons" by "close cooperating units of German and Italian air and naval forces". This was one more merchantman than the convoy contained. But more: "Remaining units are trying to reach Malta." The announcement continued: "The convoy was scattered and the greater part of the escort vessels are sailing back westward."

A special Italian announcement was more modest, but still exaggerated in claiming that one cruiser and three ships were sunk by the Italian navy, while one cruiser, one destroyer and three ships were sunk by the Axis air force. It also claimed that 32 Allied planes were destroyed while 13 Italian aircraft were missing.

The British Admiralty put out its own statement declaring that the Axis announcements were "inaccurate and no reliance should be placed on them". It added that the operation was "still proceeding and an official statement will be made as soon as practicable". Although the Axis propaganda announcements were inaccurate and exaggerated in some details, nevertheless the casualties suffered by this most vital convoy were extremely high. As well as those vessels already mentioned, the Royal Navy also had the carrier *Indomitable* and the cruiser *Kenya* damaged, while nine of the fourteen merchantmen were lost — two out of every three. To get what was left of this heroic convoy through — and 40,000 tons did arrive — over 1,000 seamen courageously forfeited their lives.

The Axis had suffered too, especially in aircraft. Of the 250 planes Kesselring was known to hold in Sicily, 66 were definitely destroyed, and another 60 most probably destroyed, while many more were damaged. The escort had also destroyed at least two submarines and two E-boats.

Five British merchantmen remained to complete the last few miles. Three forged ahead while the *Brisbane Star* was fighting her own private war, and the tanker *Ohio* was almost lost, but not quite. This, too, was a meritorious individual victory with the tanker badly holed and twice evacuated, though never abandoned. Her skipper, Captain Dudley W. Mason, who was awarded the George Cross, never gave up hope and reboarded the vessel with his men to complete the epic voyage, slowly, painfully, and with the buoyancy assistance of the Royal Navy.

It is practically certain that as usual it was small boys who first sensed the arrival at Malta of the few harassed and damaged merchantmen. Looking hard out to sea — the Maltese youngsters have fine eyesight — they were soon crying: "They're here! . . . They've arrived! . . . Santa Marija! . . . They're here!" and were rushing through the streets collecting flags and friends.

By the time the first ship of this renowned August convoy had reached the boom at the harbour entrance with guns still manned and pointing skywards and gunners still stripped to the waist, greasy with oil and sweat, there was a great multitude gathered on bastions and ramparts, rubble heaps, rooftops and roadways, waving and cheering from every conceivable vantage point. There was even a band at St Elmo Point overlooking the breakwater. Three damaged ships, the *Port Chalmers*, *Rochester Castle* and *Melbourne Star*, sailed bravely in during the evening of 13 August 1942 and under a continuous air cover of darting, searching, swooping, shepherding Spitfires.

The people gave the courageous survivors of this historic convoy a tremendous welcome, thousands cheering them in and waving banners and flags, while the old stone fortifications of Valletta and the Three Cities echoed their joy. And the cry was not a self-pitying whimper of "Now we can eat!" but rather an aggressive triumphant: "Bread for us and bombs for them!" None but the harassed inhabitants of a sea-bound, beleaguered fortress, who knew the power of intense bombing, could better appreciate the hazards and terrors of that necessarily slow voyage through mine-infested seas, beset by submarines below and bombers and fighters above.

Malta has always depended upon the freedom of the seas and merchant sailors are always welcomed but none have been entertained so heartily as the men of the surviving ships of the famous August, or Santa Marija, convoy. The Governor himself, Lord Gort, stood on the Upper Barrakka among the bareheaded, shirt-sleeved people he led as the first three ships came in and he later played host to all the captains at San Anton Palace.

The people cheered but they did not know. They counted the ships, they saw their scars, they watched the wounded being brought ashore. A woman standing next to Miss Mabel Strickland, who recalled the poignant pathos of the moment even twenty-five years later, was murmuring to herself in Maltese: "They have arrived. Blessed be God's wisdom." Three ships in. Then the people looked again to sea. Looked hard for more and saw nothing — and they knew. It is odd how even a multitude will react simultaneously. The cheering stopped. There was dead silence. The whole assembly had suddenly sensed the extreme trials of the survivors. Three only! They did not know that the *Brisbane Star* and the *Ohio* were still struggling. Three ships out of fourteen!

Next morning, 14 August, the *Times of Malta* report on the coming of the convoy contained these words: "Malta feels humble in the presence in our harbour of the ships of the Mercantile Marine . . . If the feelings of the people could be expressed in simple action, Malta's George Cross would be nailed to the mast of every ship in harbour." Malta understood.

The *Brisbane Star* arrived at midday on the 14th and the tanker *Ohio* limped slowly in another day later, early on the 15th, supported by the destroyers *Penn* and *Bramham*. Her coming coincided with the Feast of the Assumption and the end of a nine-days period of prayer to Santa Marija, Patroness of Malta, to intercede on behalf of the island and the Empire.

The following poem, written and published at the time, gives an idea of the impact of this saga of courage on the island. It was received with thunderous applause that reflected the great admiration of the hundreds of soldiers, sailors and airmen present when it was recited in the Long Ward of the old hospital of the Knights near St Elmo, Valletta, and broadcast over the Rediffusion system to the people. The concentration of such feelings about heroism, endeavour and suffering into telling lines of verse seemed to be appreciated as some relief for emotions of frustration and, in a way, helped to sustain us, as though we were looking in through a peepshow window at the dramatic happenings of another world. It gave me a tangible task and I was grateful that I could capture the mood and hopefully light, or lighten, the way. Enough.

In those days we could not mention the names of ships and, indeed, the verses had to be submitted to censorship. The aircraft carrier was *Eagle*.

MALTA CONVOY—AUGUST 1942

Battling down the Channel on a cold, wet, windy day;
Looking hard to starboard, looking hard for who can say
Where the devil fish lie lurking?
So it's double watch, no shirking,
And it's dim-dum-damn hard working
Of a passage through the Bay.

Tossing through the mountains of a rolling ocean swell,
Looking at the heavens, looking hard for who can tell
When the carrion birds may hover?
Drop their filth and turn for cover,
Like a wench to her new lover,
Riding high and raising hell.

Moving by St Vincent, by the Cape of Trafalgar
And onward to Gibraltar with the signal: "Here we are!"
There the handshake and the shipping
And the "God Speed!" come tripping;
Then it's off to Malta ripping
With an escort, fa-de-rah!

Rolling through the Medi with the porpoises at play;
Looking hard to starboard and to port, for who can say
Where the devil leaves his childer?
Will the horses blow up wilder?
Will they blitz or take it milder?
Come by night or come by day?

Sudden as the sunset in the far-off China Sea
Came a burst and blast of lightning and we saw her riding
free,
And we saw her planes go slipping,
And we knew that she was tripping
To the place where all good shipping
Sails at last — the Twilight Sea.

Silent as a brother when the funeral guests have gone;
Listening and watching, but plodding, plodding on.
Our charioteers outspreading
Their silver wings; while heading
Towards the Isle we're threading
Through the spume to pass Cap Bon.

The sunset red and glowing, the sea bright red with flame
And blood and guns and battleships and cargoships and
fame.

The Stukas diving, daring,
The sailormen a-swearing,
The barrage bright and glaring
—At eventide they came!

Steady as a trooper rolling homeward from the East,
Calmly as a file of nuns headed by a priest;
The ships in place and fearless,
The morning sun so cheerless,
Our gunners cursing, peerless.
No equal has the Beast.

Mighty is the conflict when the odds are on the foe;
Mighty is the man of war who's done and does not know.
All that day we fought them,
And with our blood we taught them,
Until the evening brought them
Time to mourn and go.

Lurking in the shadows of a dark mid-autumn night,
Dirty little sea rats with a poison bite.
By our star shells sighted,
By our searchlights lighted,
By our guns benighted,
Blasted, put to flight.

Bombers in the morning with a full, black, screaming
load,
Diving, hissing, hurtling, ugly as the toad.
All came down to get us,
Many now regret us,
None will e'er forget us,
Nor we their devil's code.

Limping into harbour with the cargo in the hold,
Sore, begrimed and bloody; steadfast, stately, bold.
Signal terse, hard bitten:
"Merchantmen from Britain!"
—One more chapter written,
But many tales untold.

The *Ohio*, which brought in 11,500 vital tons of oil, was unfit to face the sea again. She was beached and repaired sufficiently to house stores and later provided accommodation for some Yugoslav seamen. After the war she was sadly towed out to sea and sunk off St George's Shoal.

I met Captain Mason while he was kicking his heels around Valletta waiting to return to Britain. He badly wanted another ship and was angry at the delay. Like so many of us on the ground in Malta he felt frustrated at not being able to hit back personally, but unlike us he would soon be able to do so — we had to stay on. Week after week he waited, in no way thankful for the respite after his tense and grilling experience, but eventually he got his way and was flown home. He was soon back in action and in the Mediterranean. With another tanker under his feet he was delivering fuel in the North African landings and, what must have greatly pleased his aggressive spirit, on the flat deck above the oil tanks were stacked aircraft. He retired in 1958 to a cottage in Hampshire.

In 1967, on the twenty-fifth anniversary of the arrival of the Santa Marija convoy, many of these merchant seamen, officers and men, returned to Malta to hold a nostalgic reunion, to look again at Grand Harbour, Valletta, the Three Cities and the ramparts and bastions they knew so well a quarter of a century earlier. They again received a great welcome, but in happier, peaceful mood.

The arrival of the five ships of the August convoy helped to restock the nation's larder and provided some badly needed fuel to keep the aircraft offensive, but it had no immediate beneficial effect on the food ration. The high expectancy of the people was deferred. The *Times of Malta* declared in a leader on 14 August: "We must . . . place the goods which Britain has sent us in safe storage. And then on with the battle!" And in the 'Santa Marija' leader of 15 August:

The keynote remains that of conservation of supplies. The flash of enthusiasm engendered by the sight of ships unloading in harbour must not allow us to forget or ignore that the war has yet to be won. The happy fact remains that the 'Target Date' has been put off indefinitely, and we are able to withstand a far longer siege, and to continue as a vital fighting unit . . .

Note: ". . . we are able to withstand a far longer siege . . ."

Note: ". . . to continue as a vital fighting unit." No respite. Tighten belts again.

In fact, even though the 'relieving' convoy, or what was left of it, had arrived though battered and bloody, and the world thought that Malta was eating again, in the ration for the second half of August—the ration that had been only half a ration from June—there was now no issue of sugar, rice, flour, edible oil, tea, milk or toilet soap. None of these things for that fortnight. Yes, tighten belts again.

The August convoy did deliver Malta from the Axis grip that had become almost a stranglehold and enabled the island to fight on still longer in the knowledge that there was a measure of food in the larder. It renewed hope and reinforced the aggressive spirit but it did not ease the gnawing feeling in the pit of the stomach of men, women and children, nor bring them immunity from the ravages of disease.

> *O God of Courage, Hope and Right,*
> *Maintain us steadfast in this fight.*

SIXTEEN

Heroines at Home

Morale was high throughout the siege in spite of the overall devastation and the daily alarms. The troops stood to at dawn and dusk and those in defensive posts were peering over their sights at every air alert. The populace still attended their churches in the very early morning, then went about their daily tasks. Whatever destruction occurred there was an organized effort to keep the roads clear — although this became impossible in some cases — and the police did a remarkable job in this respect. There was a communal effort to keep things tidy and the brooms came out after every raid. In the village of Luqa, adjacent to the airfield, this was an almost continuous task, but even piles of rubble can be kept within bounds. Life was encompassed by devastation and much clearance and repair work must be left for a happier, easier time. "God, what a task lies ahead!"

Nevertheless, today with all its danger was not a time for despair but a time to greet one's neighbour with the new day and to be grateful that neighbour was still there. Nothing succeeds like normality, and the most normal event of the day — when there is no longer a milkman or goatherd to make his early delivery — the most normal event is the daily paper even if it is only a double sheet. There were some great difficulties to be overcome each day by every newsboy and every delivery van before the morning paper reached the reader, but the *Times of Malta*, *The Sunday Times of Malta* and the vernacular *Il Berqa* (Lightning) never failed to publish, although the presses were badly bombed twice.

These newspapers, all led by the Honourable Mabel Strickland, who was later awarded the O.B.E., played a brave part in maintaining morale throughout the siege. They kept the public fully informed and when fire from bombing burnt reels of newsprint the paper still appeared on the streets next morning — with scorched edges. Even that was a boost and a talking point, reflecting the spirit of 'we are in it together' and 'we are still in business'.

On 10 April 1942, during a fortnight of intense blitzing of the island, the Maltese flag was hauled up over the *Daily Express* offices in Fleet Street amid the cheers of London's journalists and passers-by. Reuter long quoted a cable they received from *The Sunday Times of Malta* one night during this high blitz. The atmospherics affecting the radio beams had been particularly bad that Saturday night but the cable, as understandably it might have done, did not express self-concern and absorption with the warlike activities then blasting the area. It was, however, marked 'Urgent' and said anxiously, as there was a deadline to meet: "Repeat football results!"

It was at this time of particularly high tension with the world's eyes watching anxiously and admiringly the endurance of the battered islanders that the Nigerian *Daily Times*, eulogizing the "valour, devotion and endurance of this gallant island", put forward the suggestion that the Victoria Cross should be awarded to the people. Whether King George VI took this cue or had already decided is not known but it demonstrated the universal concern and admiration and it was only a few days later that His Majesty made his historic and world-acclaimed gesture with his own special unique award.

On 23 May 1942 the journalists' weekly *Newspaper World*, published in London, declared to its writer readers:

> We in Fleet Street took legitimate pride in staying on the job and bringing out the papers when London was burning, but our ordeal was short compared with the prolonged martyrdom of Malta. The *Times of Malta* and *Il Berqa* have come literally hot from the press—their edges charred with fire. The bombing of Malta is regular. So is the production of the island's two newspapers. Not once have they failed to appear.

Reuter's truly 'on the spot' correspondent was Miss Winifred Cutajar Beck. Winnie's descriptive and dramatic despatches were praised in London and repeated in the world's Press. Five days before the award of the George Cross was announced, those hard-headed men at Reuter, so used to receiving war despatches from experienced correspondents in all theatres of operations, were yet so deeply impressed by the stories coming out of Malta that they cabled Winnie: "London 10 April 1942 stop congratulations for graphic blitz despatch which has been widely published stop thanks for efficient service in ordeal dash we salute you dash good luck stop reuter."

The whole team of dedicated reporters and photographers did a fine job to keep the people and the world informed and often took their lives in their hands to get their stories and, particularly, their pictures. Some shots of bombs exploding near Manoel Island submarine base were taken from *dghaisas* and made the reader wonder what sort of a madman would be in a rowing boat in the middle of a harbour during an air raid. Throughout the siege the newspapers echoed the spirit of the people with great inspiration and understanding. They reflected the humour, too; which was not involved but spontaneous simplicity. Like the daily joke of two or three lines in a single column box headed: "From My Parrot", which always struck home. One such: "I've got an awful stomach ache!" "You've been eating too much!" Silly today but wryly telling then.

The Maltese, loyal to the Governor, Lord Gort, and led in religion by their Archbishop, Bishop Maurus Caruana, also had a great respect for Miss Mabel, as she was affectionately known. Daughter of the late Lord Strickland, former Prime Minister who had done so much for the island, she was respected for her great efforts not only to keep the local newspapers alive through almost impossible conditions but also to maintain them as morale boosters. Not as propaganda pieces — the Maltese have 'X-ray eyes' and can see through any propaganda — but to print the truth and as far as possible the whole truth. This was particularly important when rumour flourished and when tales of devastation were sometimes overplayed. Mere rumours of Allied losses, too, could breed despondency and become exaggerated, but the truth, as Lord Gort reminded, never hurts. Miss Mabel's papers did more. Editorials explained the reasons for unpopular actions and any comment was practical, even inspirational. All this helped to maintain morale and as France's Marshal Foch once said, and the Lieutenant Governor, Sir Edward Jackson, reminded the people of Malta: "Battles are won and lost in the soul."

It was quite natural for this most Catholic people to call upon God for help, also to accept tribulation in His name. Some believed that destruction of their cherished religious architecture and prized possessions was a chastisement. When their churches fell — and some seventy churches and innumerable convents were heavily damaged — some cried: "What have we done? How have we sinned?" Not all may admit this but I have heard it cried in the agony of the moment. In simple faith there is simple love. And in love simple belief. Belief in a God who cares and therefore chastises as any father should. But this was a questing attitude not an acceptance of defeat. The people prayed with simplicity that the bombs should fall in the sea and they prayed for strength and found it. Strength of spirit as well as strength of arm and it was the spirit they gained through faith that gave them the power to endure.

On 12 April 1942, in the midst of a period of terrifying blitz raids that were coming in with 300 and more bombers at one time, the *Times of Malta* printed on the front page the whole of the verses of 'Te Deum Laudamus', 'We Praise Thee O God . . .' Surely an inspiration and true moral leadership. It was accepted by the people in no way as over-dramatic but as a natural token of their faith and feeling.

After Gort's arrival in May 1942 and his assessment of the situation, victory was still a long way ahead, could hardly be visualized, nor easily foretold. There was much to do and endure and another two years to suffer before the last air raid and the last all clear, the 3,343rd, would be heard on 28 August 1944.

The Maltese can endure much and it may be a stubborn streak that enables them to do so but when action demands it and they have faith in their leaders they can combine stubbornly for or against authority. It is a matter of justice and right. I am told that some years before the war the ferry fare across the harbour between Valletta and Senglea was one halfpenny. This was suddenly doubled to one penny but the dockies who in the early morning thronged the ferry simply refused to pay the 100 per cent increase and just walked on *en masse*. It was for justice and their rights that the nation rebelled against the French in 1798.

When war with Italy began in 1940 and heavy bombing of the harbour area was expected, exhaustive detailed arrangements were made for mass evacuation of the Three Cities. Allocations were worked out and houses in the villages were marked with the number of evacuees each could take. Only one misjudgement was made in the elaborate migration operation and it frustrated the scheme. All Malta is related and uncles and cousins are numerous and almost as close as brothers in most other countries. At the beginning there seemed to be little need to move and certainly not to billet with strangers, however well intentioned the plan. So they stayed put. But when their houses crashed around them and water and electricity services were destroyed, then they knew they must move and they did so in their thousands. The withdrawal was orderly and they chose their own destinations with relatives and friends, and they were received with Christian charity and as a natural obligation.

Much later, with the bombardment more widespread, with their whole existence in ruins, houses, convents, towns and villages demolished, family, relatives and friends killed and maimed, and living in overcrowded conditions with little light, fuel and food, it is not surprising that the people in their agony showed anger and frustration towards the double-dealing Italians. Incidentally, when I was in North Africa with Wavell's force which notched up the Allies' first victory at, around and beyond Sidi Barrani when Britain so badly needed one, and later in charge of a prisoner-of-war cage, I had found the Italians very much divided amongst themselves with a clear demarcation line between fascists and monarchists, the latter declaring resentment at being forced to fight and only too happy to be prisoners. The Maltese, battered almost beyond endurance but an extremely religious, single-minded community, now boiled over when their beloved churches were ruined and called for vengeance on Italy's pride, the Eternal City, crying "Bomb Rome!" and painted up the slogan in large letters.

Through it all the women of Malta found a new status as had the women of Britain in the First World War. I believe there was only one woman car driver in Malta when war began, certainly there was only one driving around when petrol became available towards the end of the war and she naturally attracted attention. Work for women outside the home had been frowned upon in peacetime and it was only just tolerated in war. Man alone was the wage earner. Dressmaking, nursing and serving as maids were womanly pursuits and many girls found expression within the St John

Ambulance Brigade which was to perform excellent service during the conflict.

The armed forces employed a number of girls as seamstresses and nurses. They also needed typists, clerks and cypher personnel and gradually the young women found rewarding tasks actively aiding the war effort in civil service posts, in Protection offices and with the forces.

But the housewives, perhaps, bore the hardest yoke of all. No matter how heavy the bombing they were still the hub of the home with the task of preparing suitable meals from the meagre rations with little or no fuel for cooking, in damaged homes with little or no light; often, too, in overcrowded conditions through evacuation from the towns and concentration in the villages. When the Three Cities and much of Valletta were evacuated, Balzan, Attard and Lija, known as the Three Villages, were among those flooded with refugees.

Who can live with in-laws for any length of time, especially in crowded rooms? Well, the Maltese did. Not easily, but effectively. For three or four years they strove together, uncertain about the morrow, apprehensive about each day. The women guided, tended, cared, eked out the rations and supplemented the clothing. They cooked what they could, if they could, acquired what they could, cleaned what they could—including the street every time windows and stonework shattered—queued when they should and prayed all the time. They never cried "Stay!", least of all "Surrender!" They, for their tenacity, steadfastness, love and courage, fully deserved each shining silver speck that made up the 300,000 individual tiny parts of the George Cross. Whatever the strains and tribulations, they held the families together, fully supporting their men.

THE HEROINES OF THE HEARTH

To those of our womenfolk who were killed by enemy action whilst performing the humble tasks of the home. Many who might have been evacuated to a safer area had refused to go.

Unsatisfied the man who touches fame;
Unsatisfied the freeman with his rod.
The answer to their anguish is the same:
Humility—and God.

We did not stay because we had no choice,
We did not stay to satisfy a whim,
There was no secret urge nor inner voice;
We stayed to cook for him.

We were not brave, we trembled in our fear.
We were not tough, we prayed and sometimes cursed;
And as they perished so we staggered clear
And wept, or stayed and nursed.

The raging furnace that our menfolk knew,
Knew us and with its all-devouring flame
Burnt through our strengthened souls to forge the true,
But left no name to fame.

We did not stay in answer to a voice,
We did not stay to satisfy desire;
We freely chose, and if we had the choice
We'd brave again the fire.

Unsatisfied the digger with his claim,
The wanderer with the paradise he trod;
The signpost through the ages reads the same:
Humility—and God.

SEVENTEEN

On To Victory

The Luftwaffe stepped up its offensive against Malta in October 1942 three weeks before Alamein when the Afrika Korps needed all possible reinforcements, ammunition and materials, and it was hoped to prevent or reduce interference with Axis supply lines and communications by the island's aggressive air squadrons. In the first week of October over 1,400 aircraft sorties were made against the island and the bombardment included incendiaries and anti-personnel bombs. The guns of the garrison and the defensive aircraft shot down at least 114 enemy planes but 27 Spitfires were lost although 14 pilots baled out safely. The new blitz meant that sufficient aircraft must remain 'tethered' to the island as a defensive screen but the offensive action against Axis shipping continued.

Sited before Alamein, nearly 300 miles from Tobruk harbour and 1,000 from Tripoli, Rommel was desperately short of petrol, due largely to the aggressive action that submarines and aircraft from Malta were still able to take and the casualties they were able to inflict on Axis shipping. Repeated radio signals to and from Rome were emphasizing the extreme shortages hobbling the Afrika Korps and naming relieving tankers and their movements. The cries for help were passed via Enigma, the German's secret encoding machine, considered to be absolutely foolproof. But the British had long since broken the system with their remarkable decoder Ultra and were extremely efficient in using the knowledge thus obtained without disclosing their own secret means of obtaining it. Thus, from Rommel's own despairing signals British naval vessels and aircraft were enabled to pinpoint and destroy almost all of the fuel sent to his aid at this critical period. His tactics were considerably hampered by lack of petrol as tanker after tanker was sunk at that time of intense pressure when he so badly needed freedom of movement to manoeuvre. Rommel was now reaping the effects of frustrating Mussolini when Il Duce was set to 'take out' Malta in June, while the island from its strategic position was playing its own full part in this most vital turning-point of the war.

On 23 October Montgomery struck at El Alamein and the pressure on Malta began to ease as the 8th Army took firm hold and began forcing Rommel back along the thousand miles of desert tracks and the Via Balbia to the west and his defeat. But three months after the August convoy there were still dire shortages in Malta and to ease the situation the fast minelayer *Manxman* slipped out of Alexandria harbour to make a rapid lone attempt to relieve the island. Like the gallant *Welshman* had done from Gibraltar on a number of occasions, *Manxman* got through safely and was greeted by cheers and some rather voluble, excited, demonstrative women when she sailed in on 11 November laden with dried milk and concentrated foodstuffs.

The Admiralty account of the episode records: "As she [*Manxman*] entered the Grand Harbour the population flocked to the water's edge, women falling on their knees and holding their babies up that they might see and remember all their days the spearhead of their deliverance."

Though none knew it then the fulfilment of long years of hope would not be long delayed. On 20 November four merchantmen boisterously entered Grand Harbour having come through unscathed from Alexandria escorted by H.M.S. *Orion*, wearing the flag of Admiral Sir John Power. All knew now that, with the 8th Army still advancing boldly, the way was becoming clear. When this convoy arrived there had been only twelve days' food left and the high octane fuel for the attacking aircraft was very, very low indeed, something like five days for offensive flying.

That is how close it was. A very near thing. That is what the world learned and what we gradually came to understand at the time. But it was much nearer even than that. The Governor, Lord Gort, and his able staff, by extremely careful husbandry and in the knowledge of the faith, goodwill and discipline of the nation had, in fact, already carried the island five weeks *beyond* the estimated endurance limit — the 'target date' for surrender. Five weeks that kept the island aircraft and naval vessels free to harass Rommel's supplies when he so badly needed them before and immediately after that vital period that covered the victory at Alamein. Five crucial weeks that helped to save the free world.

Royal Engineers from Egypt came with the vessels to help unload. The islanders were gaunt, tired, weak and under-nourished, but their faith had never dimmed and their spirit had never been subdued. Even now the food ration was not increased until February 1943 but there was an extra issue for Christmas. The people were tired and badly needed additional nourishment but laughed spontaneously when they heard the meagreness and the oddity of the special issue. On 9 December Mr Charles Nalder, Food Distribution and Enforcement Officer, broadcast to the nation over the Rediffusion system. In all the villages crowds gathered on the public squares, thinking with anticipation probably of turkey and plum pudding, at least of a mouthful of meat and perhaps a fruit pie to mark the festive season. The loudspeakers crackled and the announcement began: "As a special Christmas issue there will be: beans at the rate of a quarter ratal [about seven ounces] per head, biscuits seven ounces, currants $3\frac{1}{2}$ ounces and sugar at seven ounces per head." Beans and biscuits! But listen! "There is one other special item. In general to brighten the proceedings during Christmas week we will make an issue of candles — four candles and eight night-lights per family." Silence! Beans and candles! The Maltese roared!

With this November convoy a long-delayed mountain of mail began trickling in. We had all heard of it being stacked alongside the quay at Alexandria and growing bigger and bigger as the months passed. Now it began to arrive including parcels for me, from my wife Edythe in Durban — evacuated from Palestine to South Africa with other Hampshire Regiment families in 1940 — and from my brother in America. Leslie's parcel was simple and to the point, a large, rich fruit cake made at one of Schraffts' famous restaurants in New York of which he was manager. It had been with a mass of Malta mail in that quayside stack for eighteen months but the brandy or rum, I forget which, in that Schraffts' recipe had preserved it and it tasted just grand.

Malta's relief was such welcome news, even in the United States, that my 'thank you' cable to Schraffts made the New York *Daily News* in Ed Sullivan's noted column. Earlier, on 18

August, writing of "this speck of an Island", the *New York Times* had said: "That Malta stands, isolated and interminably bombarded as it is, is one of the miracles of the war." Amen to that.

Later, in 1945, the same paper was to declare:

> Malta held out when the Mediterranean was so dangerous that supplies for the British 8th Army were being carried around the Cape of Good Hope. One would think it might have been taken by paratroopers and glider troopers, as Crete was. The attempt was not made. The island remained unconquered, a light and a symbol. If we want to find the spot where the tide began to turn, Malta is as good a spot as any.
>
> If the British had been capable of surrender, they would have surrendered there. If they had surrendered there Mussolini might still be in Rome and Hitler still free to wash his red hands in the waters of the English Channel. The United States might be fighting a defensive war. But the flame did not go out. It spread.

When the 1,000th enemy plane was brought down by Skewball Beurling on 13 October the *Daily Telegraph* in a leader declared: "This sea Stalingrad has destroyed an entire enemy air fleet," while in New York the United States' Rear Admiral John S. McJaine said in a broadcast: "The defence of this vital base constitutes a performance which history will long remember. The fighting lads of the Royal Air Force and the Fleet Air Arm have won lasting admiration."

It was about this time that I talked a few strips of newsprint out of a friendly editor. He was reluctant to part with even a tiny amount of such a scarce commodity, as paper of any kind was difficult to acquire. The few sheets I was given were thin, absorbent, narrow and rather long. My brother replying to a letter said how sad it was that we were now reduced to writing on toilet rolls! Alas, toilet rolls were right out of supply.

The 8th Army continued to advance westward taking Bardia, Tobruk, Dernia, Benghazi, Sirte and were on the way to Tripoli. Their rapid advance was well supported by Royal Navy bombardment all along the coast and they careered along at breakneck speed, giving the Boche no rest from Alamein to El Agheila, 800 miles in twenty-one days. Raids on the island were not so intense now Rommel's Afrika Korps so desperately needed all the local air support he could get. The people of Malta were beginning to believe that the light at the end of the long tunnel of siege restrictions might soon be showing. As they had had sympathy with the men and women of the British Isles during their stern testing times, so they also appreciated 8th Army's glorious efforts and applauded their successes.

TALE OF THE DESERT RATS

We footed it, we slogged it,
We chased the Boche and flogged it;
But most we did in army trucks,
He ran so bloomin' fast.
And when we tried to pin him down
The blighter did the Iti brown
And left him to defend the town
Or campsite at the last.

We pounded him, we flayed him,
We caught him and we slayed him;
And when we got him in the net
He couldn't well get out.
We chased him through the burning sands
On bully beef of various brands
And now and then he'd make his stands
Which ended in his rout.

We fought him where we found him,
And every time got round him;
Which made him lift his sticks and run
For ever to the west.
From Alamein to far Matruh,
Barrani, Derna, Sirte too;
Till Tripoli came into view
We gave no rest, no rest.

We're chasing, still we're chasing,
We're pounding while he's racing.
We're building up in Tripoli
And looking 'cross the Bay.
While on towards the Mareth Line
The bombers bomb, the starshells shine
— They say the weather's clearing fine
In Malta, 'cross the way.

The spontaneity of the Maltese people was never more ably nor happily demonstrated than on 23 January 1943 when the B.B.C. announced: "It has been officially stated that Tripoli is in our hands." At once there was a rummaging through drawers and cupboards for flags and bunting that had not been seen for more than two years. Balconies were decorated, flags run up, bands played and the populace gathered in the villages throughout Malta and Gozo. The next day, being a Sunday, large groups of people began walking into Valletta from outlying villages at a very early hour and hundreds attended mass at St John's co-cathedral in the city. Soon the devastated, bomb-blasted Kingsway was thronged with a happy, chattering mass of civilians moving back and forth as in the old festa and carnival days before the war. Soldiers, sailors, airmen and policemen were caught up in the joyous atmosphere and made to join in the celebrations. The two Valletta bands, normally tense rivals, combined and marched up and down the decorated streets.

A group of boys gathered as many flags of the Allied nations as they could find, together with the red and white flag of Malta, and marched to the Palace Square. Here they paraded opposite the Main Guard where a few months earlier Lord Gort had handed over the George Cross. While the bands played the Maltese anthem and 'God Save the King' the youths solemnly and gracefully dipped their flags in salute to a great burst of applause from the huge crowds in the adjoining roads and on the balconies around the square.

The air-raid siren sounded and the guns began firing but the crowds remained to celebrate the 8th Army's victory. All the towns and villages throughout the land continued their rejoicings and in Hamrun an effigy of Mussolini was hanged and then burned. An all-too-true forecast of what later did happen to Il Duce and his mistress.

Merchant ships continued to get through to the island and in February 1943 the food ration at last was increased. On 30 March the Hampshire, Dorset and Devonshire Regiments departed for Egypt as the 231st Brigade, but in Malta they were always known as the 1st Malta Brigade and the word 'Malta' continued to be associated with their number wherever they fought. After the war each of the regiments in common with the eight others which withstood the siege, was awarded the battle honour 'Malta', and the Hampshires, for their wide-spread meritorious endeavours in many campaigns, were designated 'Royal'. During their two years in Malta the Hampshires had suffered twelve killed and twenty-seven wounded and had been awarded an O.B.E., a Military Cross and had many Mentioned in Despatches. Their tasks, their casualties and their awards were typical of every regiment on the island. They had been on duty continuously throughout their twenty-five months in Malta. The Band of the Queen's Own Royal West Kent Regiment came down from Luqa to the Grand Harbour and played the regimental marches as the Brigade sailed out. The watching Maltese could read the signs: easement for the island and somewhere there was to be a building up. In Egypt the Malta Brigade had to be fed, fattened and trained for hard aggression and their time to hit back was to come in barely three months.

In the House of Commons on 3 March 1943 the First Lord of the Admiralty, Mr A. V. Alexander, presenting the Navy Estimates, said:

> The gallant island of Malta has been sustained and relieved. Since the beginning of 1942 our operations for that purpose, including the reinforcement of the Royal Air Force in the island, cost us the loss of three cruisers, nine destroyers and two aircraft carriers, in addition to merchant ships. In view of the great history of the contribution by Malta, the Royal Navy were very glad to render that service. With the help on two occasions of a United States carrier, our aircraft carriers carried altogether 744 fighters for Malta.

And Malta was grateful for the vast and unceasing efforts of the Royal Navy.

Meanwhile the 8th Army still moved westwards along the North African seaboard and the 1st Army with the Americans closed in fighting towards the east. On 12 May the Afrika Korps capitulated and 291,000 Germans and Italians were unable to escape northward across the Mediterranean to Italy. Malta, which had harassed their lines of communication so long, now barred the way to evacuation. Rommel might still have held on for some months around Tunis but the Mediterranean Fleet and Malta-based aircraft could keep his supplies away. The Maltese exalted that the aggressive policy was at last paying off and that their own belt-tightening efforts and sacrifices had not been in vain.

On 20 June, barely a month after the rout of the Afrika Korps, before Sicily was invaded by the Allies, and when Malta was still the most forward front-line outpost, His Majesty King George VI visited the island in H.M.S. *Aurora* and was cheered wherever he was sighted. He spent ten hours on the island that had been so much in his thoughts and toured it from end to end, driving along main and country roads, through towns and villages, walking through devastated areas inspecting the damage and meeting the people. The roads were lined with applauding spectators throughout his visit and troops even in remote country areas went to the main roads to salute their monarch as he passed. His Majesty went on to visit the 8th Army in North Africa, then concentrating on preparations for the invasion of Europe.

In the latter part of June and early July much clearing of rubble was undertaken and a great deal of it was dumped into the head of Msida Creek immediately in front of the parish church which in those days had its own mirrored reflection in the sea. The creek was filled in and the area made flat. The local inhabitants merely assumed that it was one way of disposing of some of the great mass of debris that had accumulated in vast amounts all over the island.

However, on 9 July a number of landing craft suddenly appeared and tied up to the new hards. Scots soldiers also were in evidence, but they were silent, fully equipped men who kept to themselves like a well-disciplined army in transit, seeking rest and awaiting the word to strike. Indeed, they were part of the great Anglo-American force poised in North Africa, and now also in Malta, to reinvade Europe through what Churchill called its 'soft underbelly'. And there was nothing soft in the way that great warhorse and world statesman had growled it.

That day, although we knew it not then, Lord Gort had sent a signal to Egypt to what he still called the 1st Malta Brigade wishing them good fortune in the coming battle in their special role as Montgomery's independent brigade group. I have no doubt that Gort on this day thought back to the time of his arrival in Malta when he had vowed to himself that he would take what remained of the garrison and create what havoc he could in Italy's toe rather than meekly surrender the island.

That evening from their operations room in Valletta Generals Dwight Eisenhower and Bernard Montgomery anxiously watched the weather reports. I sat with the Naval Boom Defence Officer, Lieutenant Commander 'Davy' Jones, in the bar of the Command Fair for most of that fateful night. There were only about four of us there. 'Davy' had a part to play in reporting the weather pattern from the harbour entrance and disappeared every half-hour to take readings and feed the details to Ike. There was a heavy *gregale* blowing and the unseasonable and extremely stormy weather looked like jeopardizing the whole venture. It was a *gregale* that shipwrecked St Paul. Hour after hour Ike studied the reports and put off the decision to strike. His was a fearful responsibility affecting the survival of the thousands of troops packed in 3,000 ships and landing craft assembled and waiting along the North African coast and also at tiny Malta. Any delay might sacrifice the surprise factor he now held. The world, and particularly the Russians, had waited anxiously for two years for the opening of a second front. It would most naturally come in north-west Europe and the Russians had repeatedly called for just such an invasion, but this southern strike could well imbalance the Axis, topple Italy and give the Allies a great advantage.

Waiting, watching and wondering, one felt like a phantom on the sidelines of history. We knew today, the world would know tomorrow when the nations awoke to a reality accomplished. I had had this feeling before in December 1940 when the Mersa Matruh Brigade held a position at night outside Maktila at the beginning of Wavell's surprise desert advance. Then even the comrades and commanders we had left behind in Matruh did not know that a great clash with the enemy was about to begin. They thought our force was merely carrying out a repeat practice of an operational manoeuvre after, it was said, the original had been botched. We thought so ourselves until we were well into the desert and were given our attack orders. At Maktila, as 8,000 demoralized Italians led by their general streamed out to surrender to our small brigade force of about 1,500 men, I there had that fleeting thought perhaps of exhilaration: today only we know, tomorrow they will know at home. At that time Britain so badly needed a victory.

So on this Malta night of the *gregale* it looked very much as though the winds were too high and the seas too rough for the venture to go forward. Nevertheless, as the night wore on there was some easement and eventually, in spite of still stormy conditions, the order was given to move and the invasion of Sicily went in. This was a moment for which the Allies had long been waiting, a moment of history. As the morning broke the *gregale* eased, the light of day showed the hards clear again. Malta knew then and silently rejoiced.

The aircraft that roared and droned over the island that day were racing north. Hour after hour, wave after wave, they came in to refuel and rearm and raced north again. The islanders felt deep satisfaction that the invasion operation had been controlled from this outpost that had so long been on the receiving end of the Axis sword. They were also grateful and proud that of the 1,200 aircraft that gave protection to the 3,000 ships of the invasion armada, some 600 flew from Malta. Air Chief Marshal Sir Keith Park who controlled the air operation also used 600 planes based in North Africa. General Eisenhower later signalled to Sir Keith: "Except for the Malta air forces . . . the attack on Sicily could scarcely have been classed as feasible." So different from the days of endurance when we had only six Wellingtons . . . now five . . . now four . . .

MONTY IN MALTA
On the eve of the invasion of Sicily, 9 July 1943

ARRIVAL OF THE FORCE
Gathered a force in a night as of travellers resting;
Quiet and steadfast and fit and of bearing assured.
Firmly and quickly encamped, calm and cheerfully jesting;
Keen for the struggle ahead, to all hardship inured.

THE COMMANDER
Neither the weight of the years nor the cares of past battles
Enfurrow his brow as he quietly walks with his men.
Rather the litheness of youth all prepared for war's rattles;
The confident leader of craftsmen from highland and fen.

THE MEN
Here not obedience blind nor fearsomeness straining,
Here not the 'Yes men' with sudden exuberance swaying.
Here not the madness of lust nor foul wantonness straying,
Here but the calmness of trust and the faith in his training.

Theirs not the goading of duty, unreasoning blindness;
For them not the raping of beauty, nor promise of kindness.
Rather the knowledge of right and uprightness, humility;
Knowing their strength and their weakness, their fitness,
                                                    ability.

AND SO THEY PASS TO BATTLE
Travels a force in the night, full of confidence burning.
Quiet and steadfast and fit and with spirit aglow.
Carrying strong in their hearts the deep thoughts of our
                                                    yearning
"God Speed!" both for us and their kin — who tomorrow
                                                  will know.

Our thoughts were, too, with those regiments that had
been among us, the Hampshires, Dorsets and Devonshires of
the Malta Brigade. We knew they were somewhere out there,
perhaps already landed. We knew what their thoughts were
when they were frustrated among us on the besieged island.
We thought we knew what they must be feeling now.

SONG OF THE MALTA BRIGADE

When we had to go a-scrounging for a mite of rotten wood
To get the blitzed-out soyer on the boil,
And we shared our bit of bully ('twas the only thing we
                                                    could)
With the kids who came to help us with our toil;

When we swopped a bit of *rooty* for a basinful of spuds,
Though the sergeant's watchful eye was all around;
He was pretty mighty careful that we didn't sell our grub,
But appreciated anything we 'found';

When we never had a chance to get a spot of leave in town,
And we didn't much desire it anyway,
For the Boche gave three shows daily and at night he'd
stick around
Till we'd given him our usual 'Brock's display';

When we wished the wish of fighting men to all those Jerry
planes,
And to Kesselring a special gem we sent,
Then we vowed: "In our aggression, when we're taken off
the chains,
He'll regret each little effort that he's spent."

When we lived on next to nothing and had half as much of
sleep
And the guns were hot from dawning until dark,
Then we swore there'd be no holding us when once they let
us leap,
And our bite would be far deadlier than our bark.

But just why d'you think I've mentioned this and brought
the past to light?
Just why should I remember history?
Why? . . . *We're moving, moving, moving and we're
packed in mighty tight
In a landing craft that's bound for Sicily!*

On 27 November the war leaders of the three principal
Allies, Prime Minister Winston Churchill, President Roosevelt
and Marshal Stalin, met for talks at Teheran. Ten days earlier
Churchill had arrived in Malta aboard the battleship *Renown*
for his own preliminary British conference. Suffering from a
cold, he hardly left the ship except for a tour of the dockyard,
but the Service chiefs lived ashore and took meals in the Union
Club in Valletta. This had a famous painted ceiling which had
so far survived the bombing. It was in a room on the top floor
which had been set aside for the senior officers. General
Jumbo Wilson was particularly fortunate when at last a large
roofing slab was dislodged by a bomb and dropped with a loud
crash one morning at the place he had just vacated at the
breakfast table.

After the talks between Allied leaders in Teheran, North Africa and Cairo, Malta was honoured by the arrival of another great world leader. On 8 December 1943 Franklin D. Roosevelt, President of the United States of America, came in person to present to the island his great democracy's own appreciation of the Garrison's and People's successful, meritorious and arduous stand in defence of freedom. He gave into the hands of the Governor, Lord Gort, his own citation of honour addressed to: "The Island of Malta, its People and Defenders" — the greatest award his country could bestow. And by personally handing it over, the greatest gesture he and his people could make.

Italy surrendered officially on 8 September 1943 although the document was secretly signed on 5 September. The fact was of satisfying significance to the Maltese who had been threatened with absorption and extinction by Il Duce, had suffered bombardment and siege by the vastly superior forces of two war-rampaging nations, and had yet survived to witness the downfall of their bragging giant tormentor. The date was of special significance, too, for 8 September was the Feast of Our Lady of Victories and already Malta's National Day when the islanders commemorated and celebrated the defeat of another world-ambitious marauder who had tested their strength nearly 400 years earlier. Now the reduction to size of Italy, linked as it was to this date, could never be forgotten.

The single, but perhaps most historic, act that probably gave the Maltese their greatest satisfaction occurred on 12 September 1943 when the Italian Fleet sailed in to surrender under the bastions and ramparts of Valletta. This date, too, was significant. The fortress had been built after the first great siege of 1565, the raising of which is celebrated annually on 8 September. In fact, although this is the day historically accepted as the date of their defeat, a part of the Turkish force was still on the island and moving towards St Paul's Bay and their ships. They set fire to the village of Attard, some miles inland, before embarking on 12 September to sail from Malta's shores the following day. So 12 September was doubly significant.

The Italian sailors were in their best ceremonial dress offering full respect to the victors, but *en route* from Italy the fleet had been diverted by a German signal which enabled the

Luftwaffe to bomb and harass them. The German aircraft furiously attacked the fleet and did its best to prevent the handover. The flagship *Roma* was sunk and other vessels heavily damaged, but the twenty-eight warships that reached Malta were a grand and satisfying sight in Maltese eyes.

A fitting end to a mighty siege, which fills gold-lettered pages in Malta's book of destiny. Here was an island that had been isolated, almost subdued, but had never lost faith nor hope, and with determination had endured and survived. An island, with an aggressive-minded garrison, which had played a great part in gnawing away at Axis supply lines and had in the end become the forward outpost of retribution from which the invasion of Europe had been directed and from which the Royal Air Force had supported the landing force. Had the people wavered in their resolve during the years of siege, had their stamina not allowed the food to last just long enough, Malta would have fallen and Italy survived, with all the consequences of Axis expansion that that would have entailed. Once more the strategic position of tiny Malta had made her the 'bride of destiny', or the David with the ability to beat Goliath. But it was more than the island's position in the middle of the Middle Sea, it was something in the honey-coloured limestone rock that put the grit in the belly of a people who love freedom and have no intention ever of giving up their own particular way of life, their island, or their ever-dramatic destiny.

REPAYMENT

Yes, we have seen it,
The raging fire of crashing, roaring Mars,
The drifting flares that shone, outshone the stars,
The shuddering earth that vomited the slain.
Yes, we have seen the pain.

Yes, we have known it,
The bitter hatred for the bomber crew,
The raw primeval hate that grew and grew,
The while our dearest one by one fell back.
Yes, we have known the rack.

How to requite it?
With bright fear-reddened eyes, nerve-nodding heads
Born of our impotence and empty beds,
And with the hatred that we knew that day,
Shall we requite, repay?

Or shall we leave it
To their own consciences, which yet shall spate
And view with horror their souls' stricken state;
While we rebuild with thankfulness and zest?
Come! Let them seek their rest!

EIGHTEEN

Backward Glance

The spirit of the people. It was the spirit of the people invisibly and indivisibly intermingled with the high morale of the garrison that saved Malta and ensured the successful defence of this Mediterranean outpost of Europe and thereby enabled the Axis to be halted in Africa and then cast back upon itself through Sicily and Italy. In war and battle there are many facts and figures to be weighed and considered: the number of men and guns, the availability of ammunition, reinforcement, supplies, food, defence. But if material assets were the sole criterion the result of the conflict could be deduced as the simple answer to a perhaps complex sum and there would be no reason to join battle.

There is another factor, the spiritual consideration, that the unjust neglect or decry at their peril. The stark facts in 1940 were that Britain was isolated, under horrific attack and with her back to the wall. France was already subdued and occupied, while her forces in overseas Mediterranean territories were not prepared to fight on against the Nazis and thus contravene orders from Vichy. Italy was cock-a-hoop, bouncing with false pride, pretended ability and hopeful exploitation and reward, and ready to pounce and plunder. Nazi Germany was all-victorious and with the materials and the men to expand and conquer further. They, too, had the overwhelming desire to overrun and expand into a dictatorial empire, having built up a formidable war machine.

The cold figures as far as equally isolated and tiny Malta was concerned included the meagre resources of the island, the inability to feed itself, the largest ever population within a besieged fortress, a tiny garrison, a shortage of anti-aircraft guns and, for defence in the air, just three obsolescent biplanes left on the island by chance. There was the difficulty of reaching the island, supplying and building up the defences and the larder. Also, here was a peace-loving people undesirous of a military life, who would not take kindly to conscription.

Facts and figures should have decreed that Malta was indefensible, that control of the Mediterranean was beyond Britain's power and that all possible resources should be concentrated nearer home — in and around the British Isles. Facts and figures could have proved then that the Axis must win, certainly that Malta must fall, and quickly. Mussolini believed it and boasted. He looked at the facts, cast his lot with what appeared to be an unbeatable addition of figures and expected to expand his colonial empire with Malta the first easily-won acquisition.

But the British have always taken one other thing into consideration. They have needed to, being so often initially outnumbered and outgunned. They have relied perforce upon the spirit of the people, conscious of the rightness of their cause, aware of their necessary duty, fed by spiritual power, sustained by faith. It is men who win battles, not guns. Tanks can destroy, bombs can blast, but individuals of the infantry must occupy, exploit and hold. Against the overpowering weight of an attack that it seems impossible to resist, men still hold fast to weaken the will of their enemies with fear of what may befall them if they persist. Had guns been the deciding factor in Normandy in 1944 the German 88s in their almost impregnable and unassailable positions in the bocage country would have continued to contain the British at Caen. They had the power and the positions. Had bombs, the modern equivalent of far-reaching guns, been the deciding factor, they would have won for the Axis the Battle of Britain and the Battle of Malta. Had weapons been the deciding factor, what mathematically minded bookmaker would have backed the Malta David against the German–Italian Goliath? Even after the arrival of the Hurricanes?

All great commanders have known it was men not weapons that in the end — and in the beginning — win battles. Henry V at Harfleur, Marlborough on the long, harrowing march to Blenheim, Pétain at Verdun. Wavell with his limited resources in the vast Middle East command knew it well. Alexander, too. Montgomery made sure he got as much as possible of the armour and the weapons his men required; but he knew above all that the spirit of the fighting man was the real driving force and he brought his personality to boost theirs and so enlarged their characters and their morale individually and *en masse*.

Dobbie knew it, too. Perhaps better than many have given him credit for. As a sapper, whose life's work was concerned with building and destroying defences, he knew full well the weaknesses of the Malta garrison and the island's vulnerability. He knew how hard the task would be with all the shortcomings to overcome. The British have always realized that spiritual values outweigh all else in the last resort, and lift the soul to sustain the body and carry the individual and the nation through the crises of national disasters. Dobbie explains something of this in a foreword he wrote in 1944 for a booklet prepared from official sources on 'Britain's Conquest of the Mediterranean'—a victory that could have seemed impossible just four years earlier. In it he explains something about Malta, too. He wrote, *inter alia*:

> The Mediterranean Epic . . . has shown conclusively that . . . it is the man and the spirit of the man that matters, and that victory and deliverance are still as ever in the gift of the Almighty God. Battles are not won nor are campaigns decided by a mathematical calculation of material resources of the two opposing sides. Important as these things may be, there is still an incalculable factor which is more important than any other—and that is the spiritual.
>
> Our resources in the Mediterranean when France fell out of the war and when Italy came in against us were hopelessly, even ludicrously, inadequate . . . Our position in the Mediterranean was indeed parlous, and it became more so as the situation there deteriorated owing to the advent of German forces and to the consequent loss of Greece and Crete. Truly the mathematical calculation to which I have referred would have proved to us and to our enemies that we could not maintain ourselves in the Mediterranean, and that we must retire from that theatre or surrender every vestige of responsibility there. No doubt our enemies thought we would do so, and it was probably on the strength of some such calculation that Italy ventured to enter the war. We, however, thought otherwise, and determined to fight on and face the overwhelming odds.

Later in the same foreword:

> The impossible has been achieved. Disaster and defeat have been turned into victory, and while acknowledging wholeheartedly the splendid spirit, endurance and courage of all who played their

part yet we are forced back on the conclusion that "if it had not been the Lord Who was on our side" the impossible could not have been achieved.

He continued:

> It was my privilege to witness these amazing happenings from the vantage point of Malta, which was destined to play a great part in the epic struggle. It is possible that the importance and the role of that island fortress have only been imperfectly understood until recently, but it is very evident now that its importance was so great and its role so vital to our well-being in the Mediterranean that its retention in our hands justified any effort and any sacrifice however great. It is no exaggeration to say that the security of Malta reacted very definitely on the safety of Egypt, and all that those words imply. If Malta had fallen, the safety of Egypt would have been very gravely endangered. It was from Malta that the attacks were launched by sea and air on the enemy's lines of communication between Italy and North Africa. By means of these attacks we were able to exert some influence on the effectiveness of the enemy's forces in North Africa, and in this way to reduce the threat on Egypt.

On Malta's weaknesses he said:

> Our resources were meagre enough. Especially in the early months of the Italian war, the garrison was unbelievably weak both in men and material, and the enemy undoubtedly knew exactly how weak we were. Our air resources in Malta were practically nil, although the Fortress was only a few minutes' flying away from the many air bases in Sicily and Southern Italy at the disposal of the strong Regia Aeronautica. No wonder the Italians had been boasting that they would overrun the island within a few days of the declaration of war. Their resources were amply adequate to justify them making the attempt, especially in view of our own weakness. But this attempt was never made (just as the attempt to invade Britain was never made), and all other attempts during the two long years and more to reduce the Fortress by other means failed.
> We acknowledge with admiration and gratitude the way the people of Malta, the three fighting services and the Merchant Navy faced the ordeal and willingly paid the price needed to keep Malta safe. But even so the fact that Malta is today [1944] still in British hands is a miracle. The Miracle of Malta is a part, and a big part, of the Mediterranean miracle.

General Dobbie acknowledged the hand of God in the Malta miracle. He was himself an instrument in raising and maintaining the spirit of the people that helped to mould the miracle. Had Dobbie in the beginning considered only facts and figures of men and materials, his first consideration must have been to preserve the vast population intact when the Italians came to occupy. Had Gort, when he arrived in 1942, believed the assessment apparently intimated to him, that he might be required to negotiate the capitulation within a few weeks, and had he been content to rely only on facts and figures, he too might have been prepared only to think of self-preservation for the populace. Both men were not only great soldiers but great in their appreciation of spiritual values. Both knew that men not guns are the real deciding factor in battle. They knew, too, that in Malta men, and women, possess that great faith and immortal spirit to enable them to reach to, and to attain in good time, whatever goal they cherished — in this case preservation from a tyrannous, domineering dictatorship that was threatening to enthrall the world.

Some say they stayed and suffered because there was nowhere to run to — but they did not want to run. They could easily have revolted to throw in their lot with Italy. They did not wish it. They have never been anything but Maltese.* They accepted the Knights as protectors; they voluntarily became part of the British community of nations. They repulsed the Turks and threw out the French when they interfered with their accepted way of life. They endured the Great Siege of World War Two in the belief that their destiny lay within a free world and that their part was to aid the defeat of the oppressors.

Malta was fortunate in having two successive Governors in her hour of destiny (in reality, long agonizing years of endurance) who could recognize in the nation that spirit which

* A leader in the *Times of Malta* of 19 February 1942 strongly refuted Mussolini's often repeated insinuating claims that the Maltese were Italian by race and sympathy, that Malta was an integral part of Italy and vital to the control of 'Mare Nostrum'. The leader writer emphasized: "The Maltese are not and never have been Italians; neither have they ever been under Italian rule. The Maltese people trace their descent from the Phoenicians whose residence in Malta dates from 1500 B.C. — a long, long time before the she-wolf reared the founders of Rome."

transcends the possible against odds. Both had the ability to inspire the people to greater heights of resistance and endeavour, developed through character, supported by faith. Both men were quiet spoken, straightforward, without bombast or domineering presence. They went about their tasks quietly and efficiently, moving among the people, sharing their troubles and always approachable.

Bombs are levellers of class as well as houses; palaces fall as easily as farms — and in Malta they did. But that was not the reason for the Governors' understanding. When the petrol shortage was most acute and the working populace footsore, buses being reduced to a skeleton service, Gort moved around on a bicycle, almost unnoticed, in spite of his great responsibilities. In effect, both he and Dobbie were humble men who could gauge the spiritual power in their fellows and who knew there was no limit when true faith built and sustained a national spirit of determination to see the matter through against all vicissitudes and setbacks. A belief that in the end right would succeed, God would not let His people go. Yes, the excellent spirit of the people was the factor that saved Malta and brought glory through the agony they endured; a factor which His Majesty King George VI understood so well and rewarded with his Cross.

> For the spirit that lives in the soul that soars
> Was living then — it must not sleep!

NINETEEN

Sahha!

Today the Maltese islanders are still concerned with survival. Thirty-six years after the dire days of destiny of 1942 they are building a self-contained nation dependent to a large extent on tourism. They are still the happy, friendly people who stood so rigidly together four-square with the garrison to defend their homeland in the dark days of the blitz and the black winter and they are striving now to progress in an economic world that can and does strike down the mightiest.

In the middle of the middle sea they still see life with mixed vision, a fight to survive and a time to enjoy. Why should not one enjoy what one fights to achieve? Nor still enjoy life while one strives to a goal? Their enjoyment includes welcoming and entertaining family, neighbours, friends and those who pass close like Paul and Luke in the great storm and we Poor Bloody Infantry, gunners and airmen and sailors of the great siege.

The Maltese have a happy way of life. We who knew them in adversity most dire are grateful that they can still enjoy and strive to build on that freedom we all fought for and which they have struggled so hard throughout the centuries to retain.

Some of us return again to say "Xhem!" and are treated with the old courtesies. We still encounter the "Not to worry, Joe" sympathetic attitude. Some of us have only memories—which will long endure. For the experience, the friendship, the strength we found, we offer thanks. Those of us who do not return still remember Mother Malta. From near or far we whisper that Maltese word of farewell which is as soft as a lover's promise and full of the hope of speedy return:

Sahha!

TWENTY

Just for Remembrance

Here are a few more of the verses we knew during the Great
Siege and which, some said, helped us through.

TRYST
*(When I meet you by the fountain
a thousand years from now.)*

How long have you loved these age-old steps?
How long have you watched this rippling sea?
Do you remember the vigil you kept
A thousand years ago with me?

Do you remember the swooping birds?
Do you remember their devilry?
In the depth of my fear your heartening words
Refreshed my soul in its agony.

The crashing palaces, rubble and dust;
The noise, the smoke, the rushing of feet.
Now they are gone, the Hun and his lust.
Do you remember the bomb-wracked street?

Out of the dark, those days of strife
Are vivid again when I look at your hair.
Do you remember how sweet was life
And our thankfulness when we greeted there?

Bomb-dust and rubble, crashes and roars—
What are they now but a memory deep?
But the spirit that lives in the soul that soars
Was living then—it must not sleep.

NIGHT EPISODE

By the light of the waxing moon last night,
While the searchlights were groping and bombs burst around,
While the guns and Bofors cracked and blazed,
I heard his voice from the ground.

It was weaker than ever I'd heard it before,
Though he never was hard and never robust;
And he said so few words ere he passed
— His mouth being filled with dust.

NIGHT RAID

'Ark at the ack-ack burstin', Bill;
Look at they ruddy flares.
It makes me think o' my old room
At Shoreditch; up the stairs
A candlestick, with shadows there
Like goblins and bears.

Where is the blighter nah, d'yer fink?
My tootsies ain't too hot.
This slit trench ain't all 'oney, boy,
I'd rather 'ave me cot.
Oi! put that blinkin' lighter aht,
D'yer want ter get me shot?

I wish those bleedin' Bofors guns
Would shoot some other way;
The bloody shrapnel's pourin' dahn
Like 'ail on Christmas Day.
Why don't old Sproggin's Searchlight Chaps
Get crackin'? What d'yer say?

Lor lummy, look! They've got 'im nah!
There goes 'is bloomin' eggs!
'E don't care where 'e chucks 'em when
'E wants ter use 'is legs.
And ther's the blindin' fighter, boy!
'E's got 'im! Swipe me pegs!

THE SOLDIER'S DREAM

Oh, for the stroke of a woman's hand
On a feverish aching brow,
And the sound of a loving, quiet voice
And the smile that is ever a vow.

In the still of the night as I slept I dreamed,
Though your voice I could scarcely tell,
Your face was clear and your movement seemed
So dear — for I knew it so well.

And I stretched my arms to embrace your form
And I ached for your answering kiss.
You slowly turned and your breath was warm
On my cheek — then I heard the hiss.

And the vision faded, the joy and the pain
Were drowned by a roar and a light.
— By the searchlight's blaze, through the pelting rain,
I went slowly into the night.

INTERLUDE: MALTA 1942

Telghat! Telghat! the red flag's up!
The bombers are coming to town.
If you wait a while you'll hear the moan
Of the ack-ack shell and the horrible groan
As a Junkers comes crashing down.

Telghat! Telghat! the red flag's up!
The danger signal's high
And into the shelter we scurry and hurry —
"Go calmly now, without any flurry!" —
Looking a while at the sky.

Telghat! Telghat! the red flag's up!
The Junkers are overhead.
The barrage is up, what a terrible din!
You must get below to save your skin,
For it's quite well known he's a rotten shot,
And he's not so hot at hitting the spot
When the barrage is up and the Hurries are out
And the Spitfires are dashing around and about.
He'll drop them quick instead.

Telghat! Telghat! the red flag's up!
His engine roar is clear.
There's a whistle, shrill — we're getting a stick —
You must get below, be quick! be quick!
— He's dropped them somewhere near.

Telghat! Telghat! the red flag's up!
The bombs are in the town.
The rescue squads are stripped to the waist;
The Junkers are smoking and heavily chased
— The red flag's coming down.

ROAD JUNCTION

They've been knocking bits and pieces
Off St Peter and St Paul,
But they just can't hit the corner of the road.
All the little bits and pieces
Would make a goodly haul
If you'd like to pick 'em up and make a load.

For the bombers came a-bombing
And get very near St Paul,
But they just can't hit the corner of the road.
It's a very vital corner
And they often hit the wall
As they drop their loads and get out *à la mode*.

I've been watching poor St Peter,
Sympathizing with St Paul;
Every time I wander by I feel the goad.
But the most of them's still standing
Looking proud about it all,
For they just *can't* hit the corner of the road.

LOVE CALL

"Because I love you, dear!"—and then I woke.
The vision faded even as you spoke.
I felt an arm about my neck and knew
That even as you loved I loved but you.

The bombs were crashing but I heeded not.
I rose and wondered at the spreading blot
They made upon the earth, but still I thrilled
"Because I love you!" and my cup was filled.

"Because I love you!"—those the words you use,
You who can choose so much, yet do but choose
To say "I love you!" Even in a dream
Your words ring truth—I know they're what they seem.

And so in rest, dear love, our love loves on
And gives no rest 'til restless night is gone.
God! How the joyful coming home at last
Will compensate for anguish of the past.

AIR FORCE BLUE

Out of the blue, the very, very blue
You came to conquer and I fell to you.
Oh beautiful your eyes and fair your hair,
And in your tender grip a passion there.

Out of the sun, the brilliant, blazing sun
You swooped swift down ere I could turn and run;
And from the skies you leapt into my arms.
Oh, bold your heart—mine flutters with alarms.

Into the heavens I see your ship ride high
While I await your coming by and by.
Look east, look west, but fearless still press on.
Our moon shall rise when this day's sun is gone.

In the dark night I watch the farthest star
And send you prayers and blessings where you are.
Tomorrow! . . . Oh, tonight give blow for blow!
Think not of me — I would not bind you so.

ONE YEAR AFTER
(Malta blitz 1942)

Roses and summer and birdsongs;
Scent of the orange in bloom.
Silver and gold o'er the rubble
And gloom.

Of late the deep rumbles grow fainter.
The fear that was ours now is cast
On its cringing creator. Yet think on
The past.

The cities, the churches, the ploughland
Are stained with the blood of our slain.
Let history prove that they died not
In vain.

The gift shall return to the giver
As sure as their echoing lies,
Till His love has begotten a light in
Their eyes.

But let not the silence betray us;
The time for endeavour is here.
Rejoice in His care, but remember
Last year.

THE FOURTH SPRING

Stones walls and ragged grass, and *qares** blown
By these rough, roistering winds of early spring.
The carob tree a lusty baritone,
The bean and early corn their treble bring
In gentler tone.

Thrice have I known the glories of these days:
The clover and the *qares*, poppies red,
All intermingled with the moon's bright rays,
And dropping flares, the never-slept-in bed,
The bomb-dust haze.

One day I wandered to a farmer's door
Which stood beside the airfield bravely still,
But ere I reached it came a sudden roar;
The children who were laughing loud and shrill,
Are now no more.

Stone walls and blasted rock, a crumpled heap
Of building stone where stood a farmer's cot;
The smell of bombs; the donkey and the sheep
Still browsing, but the rest is best forgot.
They rest in sleep.

Again, I walked within the lonely town:
The flickering searchlights, and the shrapnel burst,
The bee-like humming as the scraps came down,
The distant splutter as the fighters cursed
And gained renown.

Are those days gone? The springs of those three years,
The cold, grim days when nature, too, forgot?
The nights of death, the creeping, gathering fears,
Our dim uplifted eyes: "Is this our lot —
The cross of tears?"

---

* *qares*: pronounced 'ah'res'. The yellow wood sorrel which grows prolifically in verdant areas in Malta and is commonly called 'the English grass', having been introduced by an English lady in 1806.

Stone walls and ragged grass, and *qares* blown
By these rough, roistering winds of early spring.
Now sing ye loud and clear a newer tone,
The prelude to a paean that shall ring
Through realms unknown.

Ye walls and ragged grass and *qares* sweet,
The bones and flesh and blood of those who fell,
This spring shall sound her trumpet and shall treat
Ye to the songs and tunes ye loved so well,
Before war's heat.

THE NIGHT SISTER

At first it was the scent of her hair
As I lay in my feverish nightmare sleep,
And then I saw it glisten there
As I floated, in fever, the deep.

The bright, bright light of the morning sun.
Was I still alive, intact and sane?
The throb was there but the fever done
And away in the depths of night was the pain.

A fantasy of the darkling hours,
She came again when the night returned.
The magic of meeting and touching was ours;
Those cool, cool hands on a brow that burned.

Away in the dark an angel form,
A light in a sea of terror and doubt.
Is she goddess or woman? Cold or warm?
I do not know — but I'm finding out.

THE REFUGEES

Dumbly they came to the chill of an English morning,
Listless and humble, fog-begrimed and sad;
Huddled together, thought benumbed past scorning,
Filthy and lousy, underfed, ill-clad.

Slowly they moved to the wet of an English quayside,
Lugging their bundles, hugging their children's heads;
Down the long wharf to the canteen on the leeside.
'Wildered their souls with the countless furling threads.

Later I saw them camped by an English village.
Large with their thanks, though simple the needs of that
band;
Hard with their thoughts as they spoke of their own loved
tillage.
Oh ye of an untrodden nation, can ye ever understand?

Oh ye of a virgin England, who have lived in freedom from
childhood,
Who have never known the lash, nor the cuff of an iron
hand,
When ye hear the new-found laughter of their children
wild in the wildwood,
Oh tell ye a tale of the hounded, that your own might
understand.

KILLED IN ACTION
(To d'E. G. C.)

While we were staid you laughed your merry way
Across life's stage, infectious, boyish, gay;
Treating all men as equals, comrades true,
You knew no meanness, humour led you through.
Wisdom you scattered with your waggish ways,
Turning to golden all life's leaden days;
Knowing no causes, leaving us to choose,
You'd clear the air of deadly, darkling hues.
Never a face but brightened at your sight,
Nor conference dull but gurgled with delight
At some bright quip. Know that your fellow men
Still call you "good old Joey" now, as then.
I have no doubt that as you passed the gate
St Peter smiled—you joked to learn your fate!

WE'VE STAMPED OUR FEET IN FRANCE AGAIN
(Written on D. Day, 6. 6. 44.)

Do you know the road to 'Wipers', mate,
The bloody road to 'Wipers',
The road from Mons to 'Wipers',
With the bodies stiff and black?
The place we left our mateys,
Those imperishable mateys,
Who're waiting there at 'Wipers'
For our coming, coming back.

Do you know the gate at Menin, boys,
The high arch into Menin,
The broken road to Menin,
And the stumbling, bleeding feet?
The refugees, the hell of it,
The anguish and the smell of it.
They're waiting, too, at Menin
For our marching, ringing beat.

There are roses now in Picardy,
And poppies red in Flanders,
The bloodied fields of Flanders,
We knew their muddied wrack.
And we've stamped our feet in France again,
And the Boche must take his chance again,
And the girls will sing and dance again,
At our coming, coming back.

We'll march through 'Popperinjee',
Through Passchendaele and Cambrai,
(The red canal of Cambrai!)
We'll make the cobbles crack.
And we'll turn the Boche's spleen again
Till the slate is somewhat clean again,
And our mateys sleep in green again,
At our coming, coming back.

A SONG OF THE EXILES

Oh sing me a song of the English trees;
   I hear them calling.
Of the morning mist and the evening breeze;
   They're calling, calling me home.
Oh what care I for the deep blue sky,
For the sun and the sickle moon?
Oh let me walk with my hair awry,
With the spit of a south-west gale in my eye,
And the sun blotted out at noon.

Oh sing me a song of the English fog;
   Damp echoes calling.
Of a burning log and a man and his dog;
   They're calling, calling me home.
Oh what care we for the blue, blue sea,
And the charms of the long hot day?
For the feel of the turf of the South Countree,
And the smell of the muffins and cakes for tea,
We'll battle it through the grey.

Oh sing me a song of the English lass;
   Red roses calling.
Of the chimes and the lanes and the English grass;
   They're calling, calling me home.
For what care we for the passion flower,
Or the slow, seductive smile?
Oh let me walk in the evening hour
Where the bluebell grows by the ivied tower
And be with my love a while.

THE HORSE OF TROY

All mankind looks on the British
As a very peculiar kind
And murmurs "The Humble!", "The Simple!"
Or "The fools with a weakened mind."
Then, because they don't understand it,
They do not believe it is true
And while they're in doubt, we potter about
And our idiocy gets us through.

We stood while the Hun rushed by us,
We stolidly marched away,
We built then with rock intending
To make a defensive stay.
We have taken our share of bombwrack,
We have staggered and stammered in pain,
We have stood with our backs to our broken shacks
And we've stumbled and stumbled again.

We stood and we waited for helpmates,
We sighed: "To attack, to attack!"
"Bomb Rome!" we cried in our anguish,
"Give us tools that we might fight back."
And now we have taken their cities
At the cost of our thousands dead,
And with bleary eyes and our head in the skies
"Oh, they were misled," we said.

And we burble aloud of "Mighty";
In praise of their fathers' days
And imperil our children's children
By our humble, forgiving ways.
We extend a hand in pity
To the tyrant bereft of his gun,
But if we'd fallen back through the wall of our shack,
Oh, what would the tyrant have done?

But the power is conceded ye, brethren,
To watch ye the tyrant's hand,
To listen always when he mutters,
To be watchful still lest he stand.
The British are noted for madness,
And the faith that we place in our foes.
The war is not won till we've sentenced the Hun;
Beware, lest he stamp on your toes!

THE LAST WISH

Take what you will when you strip me of power,
When you leave me to totter toward my last hour,
When you leave me to ponder on life that was dreary,
On life that was gay, that was good, that was cheery;
Then take what you will at the end of your scheme,
Take what you will but leave me to dream.

Yes, leave me to dream in my last waking hour
Of the things I have loved through the sun and the shower;
Though the things I have loved, that have made up my
                                                    story,
Will bring me no fame, nor lead me to glory.

*Take the foul schemer, the hated Hun
And his war-mad brood to the end of a gun
And press the trigger before they can run!
Take, take all these!*

Take the black bombers, the hectic nights,
The tumbling ruins and the crimson sights,
The dropping flares and the blinding lights.
Yes, take all these.

Take the damp shelters, the siren's cry,
The funeral toll as the hearse goes by —
But not the comrades who gathered nigh.
No, leave me these.

Take not the *qares*, the poppies, the corn,
The smile of the sun at the birth of the morn,
The green flash at sunset, the *torri* forlorn.
No, no, not these.

Not the tall steeples, the pounding bells,
Nor the cool white stones across the wells,
Nor the stories of love that the old priest tells.
No, no, not these.

Not the bright banners, the *festa* days,
The drab *faldettas*, the village ways,
Little brown boys, nor the goat that strays.
No, leave me these.

The flat-roofed houses, the tang of the sea,
The smiles of shy children are joys to me.
So leave me these and let me be,
To dream with these,
Dream, dream with these,
And pass through these
My God to Thee.

THE END

And thus the end! Confusion in his ranks,
And desolation round his hearth and home.
Pale, through our lines, the gibbering cravens come,
Denying yet their names, they cry their thanks.
So thus the haughty learn a different tone.
None act so well the coward as the bully thrown.

And we who know the misery and wrack
He forced on us through those dark, dismal years,
Remember, too, the faith behind our fears,
The strength we felt, the will to struggle back.
And we who know, know no elation now,
But glimpse the mortal fear that dampens his foul brow.

As to a bullying child we set a task,
To clear his brain and train his inner eye,
So now a task we'll set to tyranny,
That those who follow after may not ask:
"Why, being thrown, was not this fiend killed?"
But guard! For arrogance returns with bellies filled.

And we? Why yes, we've many things on hand.
We've still 'His Mimicry'* to bring to heel,
Our homes to build, the fiend to guard, the keel
Of that new ship to lay: *"The World we planned."*
And though we may feel tired, a trifle sore,
The busy man finds time to do that little more!

* The Emperor of Japan.

THE NEEDS OF THE PEOPLE

These are the needs of the People,
For these the People cry:
The glance of God in the morning,
And His kiss when they lay to die;
A sympathy with nature,
The love of a man and wife,
A comradeship of the nation,
And a true set course through life.

These are the needs of the People,
For these the People yearn:
Work enough in their manhood,
And the wherewithal to learn;
The light of truth in their leaders
And wisdom deep from their lips,
And the power to scorn with laughter
The vile with their poisoned quips.

And these are the needs of the People,
For these the People die:
The faith that they gained of their fathers,
The flag that they freely fly;
A sufficiency of freedom
With the right to a freeman's mind,
And a home and a hearth and a family,
And the trust of their fellow kind.

And these are the needs of the People,
Though these are the People's goads:
The wind and the cold and the lightning,
Hard toil and heavy loads,
The goal on the distant hilltop,
The racking, feverish thirst —
For those who have won through the torments
Are the People God chooses first.

Appendix

GARRISON ROLL CALL

These ships, units and air formations made up the defensive garrison and the offensive forces of Malta G.C. during the Great Siege of World War Two; some for part of the time only. Army strength around 30,000 including 15,000 Maltese.

Royal Navy

Force K: Cruisers *Aurora* and *'Pepperpot' Penelope* with destroyers *Lively* and *Lance*. Later augmented by cruisers *Ajax* and *Neptune* with destroyers *Kingston* and *Kimberley*.

Nth Submarine Flotilla: *Upholder*, *Upright*, *Urge* and *Utmost*.

Other warships that Malta will long remember with affection include the battleship *Warspite*, the aircraft carrier *Illustrious* and the United States carrier *Wasp*.

Cruisers: *Gloucester*, *Orion*, *Cleopatra*, *Carlisle*, *Kelly*, *Euryalus*.

Destroyers: *Wolf, Jaguar, Sikh, Havock, Hero, Bramham, Kandahar, Kashmir, Kelvin, Kipling, Legion, Jervis, Penn, Javelin, Nubian, Jackal, Jersey, Avondale, Gallant, Mohawk, Isis*.

The monitor: *Terror*.

Fast supply ship: *Breconshire*.

Fast minelayers: *Welshman* and *Manxman*.

Minesweepers: *Beryl* and *Swona*.

Submarines: *Thunderbolt*, *P35*, *Parthian*, *Regent*, *Rorqual, Porpoise, Cachalot*.

Tugs: *Ancient* and *Robust*.

Many of these names were, and some still are, borne in proud admiration by cafés, bars and buses.

There were also the Fleet Air Arm aircraft: Sunderland Flying Boat, Gladiator, Swordfish, Albacore and Fulmar with squadrons operating from aircraft carriers and Hal Far airfield.

A Royal Navy Engineer Captain, Captain H. E. (Harry) Lewis, was given responsibility for all transport and petrol on the island. As Director of Transport he introduced the traffic roundabout to Malta, the first being constructed at the foot of the Rue d'Argen at the head of Msida Creek. A naval paymaster captain controlled quarries and building material for defence, while other naval officers co-ordinated supplies and shipping.

Army

The Manchester Regiment, 8th Battalion.

The Royal Irish Fusiliers (Princess Victoria's), 2nd Battalion.

The Buffs, Royal East Kent Regiment, 4th Battalion.

The Queen's Own Royal West Kent Regiment, 2nd Battalion.

The Devonshire Regiment, 2nd Battalion.

The Dorset Regiment, 1st Battalion.

The King's Own Royal Regiment (Lancaster), 8th Battalion.

The Lancashire Fusiliers, a Battalion.

The Cheshire Regiment, 2nd Battalion.

The Hampshire Regiment, 1st Battalion.

The Durham Light Infantry, 1st Battalion.

The King's Own Malta Regiment, 1st, 2nd, 3rd and 10th Battalions.

The Royal Artillery: 12th Field Regiment, 26th Defence Regiment, 12th GOR Regiment, 4th Coast Regiment, 32nd Light Anti-Aircraft Regiment, 65th Light A-A Regiment, 74th Light A-A Regiment, 4th Heavy A-A Regiment, 7th Heavy A-A Regiment, 10th Heavy A-A Regiment (T).

The Royal Malta Artillery: 1st and 5th Coast, 2nd and 11th (T) Heavy Anti-Aircraft and 3rd Light A-A Regiments, and 8th Searchlight Battery, 4th Searchlight Regiment, RA, RMA and RE.

The Royal Engineers, including the Maltese manned 16th Fortress Company, RE.

There were also units of the Royal Corps of Signals, Royal Army Ordnance Corps, Royal Army Service Corps, Royal Army Medical Corps, Royal Electrical and Mechanical

Engineers and Army Catering Corps (both the latter formed in 1942) and other ancillary services.

Queen Alexandra's Imperial Military Nursing Service.

The Malta Auxiliary Corps which fed recruits to units.

The Malta Pioneer Group (formed 1942).

The NAAFI/EFI in uniform and under military discipline.

The Malta Home Guard which raised 3,000 men between the ages of seventeen and seventy in three days in 1940, carried out training manoeuvres with the Regular British Army, and eventually totalled about 4,500 men.

Royal Air Force

These are the names of the first air defenders of Malta who flew the Fleet Air Arm Gloucester Gladiator biplanes *Faith*, *Hope* and *Charity*: Squadron Leader A. C. Martin, Flight Lieutenants P. G. H. Keeble, P. W. Hartley, G. Burges, W. J. Woods, and Flying Officer J. L. Waters.

The Royal Air Force squadrons based on the island were:

LUQA	No. 23 from	December	1942 to	September	1943
	39	August	1942	June	1943
	40	October	1941	February	1942
	69	January	1941	February	1944
	104	October	1941	January	1942
	107	September	1941	January	1942
	108	June	1943	June	1944
	126	June	1942	May	1943
	148	December	1940	April	1941
	221	January	1943	March	1944
	227	August	1942	November	1942
	256	September	1943	April	1944
	261	August	1940	May	1941
TA'QALI	126	June	1941	May	1942
	227	December	1942	February	1943
	229	August	1942	December	1942
	249	May	1941	November	1942
	272	November	1942	June	1943
QRENDI	185	June	1943	September	1943
	229	January	1943	September	1943
	249	December	1942	September	1943
SAFI	126	June	1943	September	1943

HAL FAR	108	July	1944		
	185	May	1941	May	1943
		October	1943	July	1944
	229	October	1943	January	1944
	249	October	1943		
	283	April	1944	August	1945

No. 249 (Gold Coast) Squadron was the first to claim 100 enemy aircraft destroyed.

The dates are approximate. Some squadrons, as the above table shows, changed airfields during their stay, some more than once.

The aircraft which took part in the battle for Malta included: Wellington bombers, torpedo Beauforts, photographic reconnaissance Baltimores, photographic and fighter Spitfires, Hurricanes, Blenheims, Beaufighters, Mosquitoes, Marylands and Sunderland flying boats.

The Observer Corps, tiny, unobtrusive but highly efficient and mainly Maltese, played a distinctive role.

An entirely fictitious but highly effective character was 'Pilot Officer Humguffery', supposedly a fighter pilot in the air, who was given dummy orders to deceive the enemy when no island aircraft were airborne. 'Humguffery' was credited with his first two ME 109s destroyed when they shot each other down crying "Achtung! Schpitfeuer!" after hearing the dummy instructions to 'Humguffery' supposedly on their tails.

The women's medical services helped to staff the naval and military hospitals.

There were Maltese serving within the British Army, Royal Navy and Royal Air Force in addition to those in Maltese units.

The Malta Police Force worked side by side with the armed forces. Many Maltese civilians, including women, supported the services in various roles from cypher clerks to seamstresses.

The civilian Protection Officers and Air Raid Precaution personnel played an important part in directing, advising and assisting the civil population, especially evacuees from devastated areas.

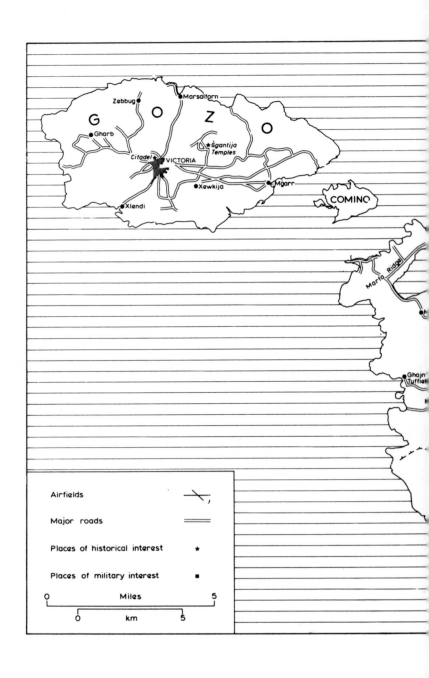

Zebbug•   •Marsalforn

G   O   Z   O

•Gharb

Citadel VICTORIA

★ġgantija
Temples

•Xewkija   •Mġarr

COMINO

•Xlendi

Marfa Ridge

Ghajn
Tuffieh

Airfields	
Major roads	
Places of historical interest	★
Places of military interest	■

0   Miles   5

0   km   5

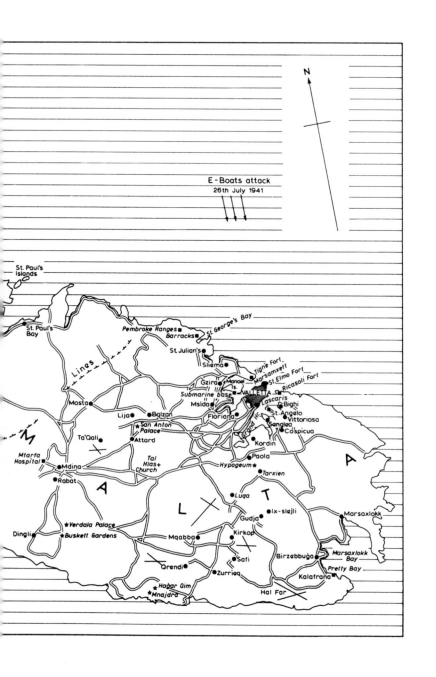

N

E - Boats attack
26th July 1941

St. Paul's Islands

St. Paul's Bay

Pembroke Ranges
Barracks

St. George's Bay

Lines

St. Julian's

Sliema

Tigne Fort
Marsamxett

Gzira
Manoel Is.

St Elmo Fort

Submarine base

VALLETTA

Ricasoli Fort

Msida

Lascaris

Bighi

Mosta

Floriana

Lija
Balzan

St. Angelo
Vittoriosa

San Anton Palace

Senglea

Cospicua

Ta'Qali

Attard

Kordin

Mtarfa Hospital

Mdina

Rabat

Tal Hias+ Church

Paola

Hypogeum

Tarxien

A

A

L

Luqa

T

Ix-slejli

Gudja

Marsaxlokk

Verdala Palace

Dingli

Buskett Gardens

Mqabba

Kirkop

Birzebbuġa

Marsaxlokk Bay

Qrendi

Safi

Zurrieq

Kalafrana

Pretty Bay

Haġar Qim

Mnajdra

Hal Far

Index

NOTE: Ranks are those held in 1940–43, though in a few cases later promotions are included. Decorations are omitted except those awarded for supreme valour — VC and GC.